VIXEN

VIXEN

VIXEN

FROM MORMON CONVERT
TO LDS APOSTATE

BY LINDSAY HELM

Elisely
PUBLISHING

Copyright © 2021 by Lindsay Helm

First paperback and hardcover editions - October 2021

Book cover artwork by Shout Out Branding.

Paperback ISBN: 978-1-0879-2024-5
Hardcover ISBN: 978-1-0879-2017-7
Ebook ISBN: 978-1-0879-1065-9

Subjects: Body, Mind & Spirit—Healing, Prayer & Spiritual | Religion—Cults | Family & Relationships—Conflict Resolution

PRINTED IN THE UNITED STATES OF AMERICA ON ACID-FREE PAPER

Published by Elisely Publishing
www.elisely.com

To Travis, for being my anchor
while I am at the helm of my ship.
For loving me unconditionally
since the moment we met.

To my mom, for showing me
how to be brave and driven.

To Beckham, for teaching me
how to love endlessly.

unorthodox
by Lindsay Helm

Angry, confused,
bitter and used.
Unworthy of love,
deemed sinner up above.

Ruffling feathers,
creating stormy weather.
Bursting from the inside out,
my soul free to express doubt.

Still grieving inside,
the sister-life that died.
And time lost to perfection,
a painful change of direction

They claimed it was a trial
that I was in denial.
After all, everything was true
in that rosy church pew.

Yet, when I left
instead of a community bereft,
I sat on the outside looking in,
wondering when the unconditional
love would begin

But I heard them loud and clear
"You're giving up eternity!" they
would jeer.
"Endure to the end,
never waiver, never bend!"

"Remember, remember,
you must put out your ember.
Sparks start fire.
Revolutions, you would sire."

"You're only good if you stay with us.
Be quiet, don't make a fuss.
Eternal salvation requires
no questions, let faith transpire!"

I'll never be good enough?
Saints bluff.
I'm a bitter fruit.
Watch me as I take my loot.

Get ready to pay your toll.
I'm too powerful to control.
Not a spark, but a flame.
Too fierce to be tame

A vixen on dry ground.
Sprinkle holy water all around.
Burn me alive, I dare you.
I will always stand true.

I'm ready now, I'm ready now!
Prepare to take your bow.
From the ashes I'm reborn,
a woman sheathed in scorn.

My armor has been made,
with the sign of the nail it was paid.
Eunice is nowhere to be found.
Anywhere, on this battle ground.

Just me,
much more scary.
I've been held captive too long.
Like a beast, I am strong.

Unbound, unleashed.
Like sister, Eve's feast.
The Fall of Adam.
Man, she really had him.

To think one woman
could cause the fall of man.
No wonder they took our power,
and locked us up in that high tower.

They threw away the key
and convinced us that's our eternity.
Watch me burn the tower down
and reclaim my righteous crown.

Get ready, get ready!
My hands are steady.
I want a show.
Let's go, let's go!

contents

contents

INTRODUCTION

vixen

*Sometimes the Godliest thing to do
is to be true to ourselves.*

Around the age of 21, Kelly banded together with her girlfriends and entered a lip-syncing competition.

Young women everywhere showed up in all their 80s big-haired glory. But not one of them had hair like Kelly. Oh no, she was a sight to behold. Her golden tower of cascading locks turned heads everywhere she went. Women approached her constantly to ask how she got her hair *so big*.

She was one of those women you love to hate, with naturally beautiful hair that was always perfect—80s perfect. She was confident, friendly and really fun. Kelly was one of those popular "baddies" who was also kind and down to earth.

In today's lingo, she was straight goals.

Kelly and her gaggle of girlfriends were extra excited about this competition they'd just entered because the reward was to die for. The reward was so big, their hair seemed small in comparison. The reward was brighter than their aqua blue eye shadow. The reward for being the best 80s lip-syncing band was… Bon Jovi.

Bon. Jovi.

Basically, the sex god of the 80s. The Fabio of rock 'n roll.

Kelly was not one to turn down a challenge, let alone one where she didn't have to sing—because to be honest, she was a terrible singer. If it were an actual singing competition requiring any vocal talent she would've been scrubbing tomatoes out of her big hair for a week after being booed off stage.

But this, *this* was a lip-syncing competition, which meant Kelly and her girlfriends just needed to know the words to the song, put on a damn good show, and look fierce doing so.

All of the things women are good at.

So, that's just what they did.

Fast forward 10 years and I had just found a box of home videos in my grandpa's closet. With young curiosity I popped a VHS with "*Vixen*" written in black sharpie across the side into the VCR.

In a few seconds a grainy video had appeared. The most beautiful and fiercest woman I'd ever seen came on stage and was dressed head to toe in black. I didn't recognize her but was immediately captivated by her beauty and confidence.

Her lace gloves held a microphone close to her bright pink lips. The crowd went wild as the music played. The woman whipped her big, blonde hair around like a rockstar on stage. She owned every inch of that room, as every single person was *completely* captivated by her. And there was not one ounce of shame or meekness in her demeanor. She was bold and brave and absolutely *killing it*.

By this point I was wide-eyed and glued to every bit of what I was seeing. A few seconds later, my mom walked into my bedroom and her eyes went big when she saw what I was watching.

"What is this, Mom?" I asked, still wide-eyed.

"Oh my God, I haven't seen this in forever!" she laughed and shook her head.

"Who is that woman?"

"Honey, that's me!" A huge smile spread across my face and I laughed. There is no way *that* is my mom!

"You were in a band?" I asked.

"Yep! Well, kind of. And we got to meet Bon Jovi!"

"Wow! That's so cool, Mom! What was your band's name?"

She hugged me close as she kept her eyes on the television—remembering her past self, so full of vivacious life. She paused for just a moment, taking it all in.

"We were called, *Vixen*."

"*Vixen*," I whispered.

Just then, the music stopped and the crowd went wild again. Louder this time. The grainy footage clicked off and the television turned to white noise. I stayed still, not wanting to take my eyes off the screen, hoping for more.

It seems to have been a lifetime since the day I found my mom's music video, and yet I remember it with such clarity. That day, I learned about taking chances. I learned that even when something is new and terrifying and the whole world is watching, I could live big and be bold. I learned that there's no reward if I don't take the leap. I learned to live in the moment and not overthink everything. I learned that the stage is whatever I make it. That I could stand up there and second guess and flounder, or I could put on my lace gloves and hot pink lipstick and do the damn thing—*my* way. I could make up the words to my *own* song.

For years after my conversion to Mormonism, I thought back to that video. "I could never do that," I would tell myself. Church culture would never stand for a Mormon woman being all... *that*. It's too much. It wouldn't invite the spirit into my heart. It wouldn't sustain the teachings of the gospel. All of her boldness

Lindsay Helm

and "not giving a shitness" was quite literally the opposite of what I had been conditioned to be. And yet, I found myself yearning to be like her in the secret aching pains in my own heart.

After leaving the church I held tight to that memory and to the girl I used to be before I converted. The girl that was on her way to becoming just like her badass mom. And I decided I wanted to be that. I wanted to have my "*Vixen*" moment. I wanted to do something scary and bold, but so full of truth and authenticity that I could leave an impression on someone, somewhere who needs the big hair courage of an 80s wannabe rocker.

Writing this book is my "*Vixen*" moment. My story is my stage. It is the VHS tape of my becoming. It is here in these pages that I have found myself—that I have become a *Vixen*.

But it took a lot of work to get here.

For the last six years I have unpacked my entire soul in search of answers to so many questions. Why do we make ourselves uncomfortable in order to make *others* comfortable? Do we do this out of love or conformity? Out of respect or control? Do we unintentionally manipulate our behaviors to receive love from others that we desperately desire? Why did I feel like my worth was entirely dependent upon what the church and its members thought of me? I wanted to understand why the church made me feel like I was giving up eternity in order to be true to myself here and now? And the biggest question, what if living *my* truth offends *them*?

This one took me a while to process through. For so long my self-worth was fed by my Mormon checklist of righteousness. My confidence came from my tight-knit Mormon community— the community I had left behind. So, when I started to show my true self, I knew some people would want to put me in my place.

They would want to shut me down, call me out, and if that didn't work, they'd tell me I wasn't good enough to begin with.

"You must not of had a true testimony," they would say.

After a while I came to understand that I wasn't offending them. I was *scaring* them. In their minds I had followed Satan down a blazing path to hell. I had let temptation lead me away from celestial glory. I had traded in my eternal life with my family for "temporary fulfillment." I'd let go of the iron rod in pursuit of the great and spacious building that is the temporal world. In their minds that was terrifying because their world is black and white. Right and wrong. Heaven and hell.

So, what I did was leave.

Quietly.

I figured if I left quietly and didn't ruffle any feathers, I could make it out alive. And by "alive" I mean "remaining in the good graces of everyone that I desperately wanted to love me." I had thought that if I left quietly and respectfully (cue in toxic people pleasing traits) they would see my proverbial horns a little less.

This is when I became an Oscar-worthy actor. I plastered on the smile, put on the dress, and hid my authentic self from everyone.

I felt this was my only choice, because in my experience love within the church is conditional on an active membership and joyful submission to everything handed down by Mormon prophets, seers and revelators—the patriarchy. That love which seems unconditional is removed the moment a person decides to leave or ask the really hard questions. That love is taken away the moment they feel you are going down the path towards Satan.

I wish that had not been my experience, or the experience of the dozens of others who have reached out after I publicly announced writing this book. But it is. Other women have shared their stories of heartache, disownment, abuse and manipulation. They've been asked for divorces, asked to move away from their families, ignored, and verbally and mentally abused by family and friends "in the name of God." Their families ignore boundaries, verbally assault, and attempt to control them, and then say, "It's because we love you."

Unconditional love doesn't work that way.

But unfortunately, the kind of love I grew up with in the church was conditional. I had it in my head all those years that to be worthy of love I had to fit into the celestial mold. In my mind the mold was the same for every female. Even though we are different, we are asked to squish and squeeze ourselves into this prefabricated idea of what women should be. The perfect mold of a mom and wife. And this molding had begun at the young age of 14.

Always be worthy of a temple recommend. Don't watch anything rated higher than PG-13 on television. Don't watch porn. Or sex in movies. At all. Don't listen to music that drives out the spirit. Don't curse. Don't skip church. Don't drink coffee or tea. Don't drink alcohol. Don't stay out late on Saturday nights, you mustn't be tired for church the next day.

Don't wear shorts or skirts above your knees. Don't wear anything that reveals your shoulders or chest. Don't wear two-piece bathing suits. Don't wear clothes that are too tight. If cleavage or lower back can be seen, change your clothes—you'll make the boys give in to temptation.

Don't date until you are 16, but really not until you are 18. Don't have sex until you are married. Don't do anything sexual at all—even with your own body—until after you are married. Sex is meant for procreation. Masturbating is a sin. Don't be alone with a male until you are 18—unless you are being interviewed about your moral and sexual habits alone in a room by a bishop, then it's okay. Help the boys and men stay righteous by being an example of Christ-like behavior.

Attend Young Women and learn how to cook, serve, and take care of others while your male peers play basketball and eat the food you make. Doubt your doubts before you doubt your faith. Endure to the end. And don't forget to pay a full tithing on your babysitting money.

You get the picture.

By the time you reconfigure yourself to fit the mold, you become a shell of a human. A disfigured porcelain doll with eyes glazed over and a painted-on smile. And if you move in the wrong direction, you shatter.

All of these "don'ts" make an already confused anxious young person even more confused and even more anxious. What's meant to give direction and stability creates high dependency and self-consciousness, which is what happened to me. Eventually the stress of these "don'ts" can lead to a change in brain chemistry. So, it shouldn't be surprising when I tell you that I struggled with extreme undiagnosed anxiety for almost 10 years, as I tried so desperately to fit into the church's mold to be worthy of love and blessings by following the rules.

Living in a world I didn't consent to caused me to become mentally unhealthy because I could no longer trust myself. I couldn't live my life in a way that would cause others to be uncomfortable. I couldn't live authentically because if I did, I would be unloved. I became faced with a choice of either being true to myself and risking relationships or staying put while my mental health slipped away.

You all know what I chose.

But as I dove headfirst into my new post-Mormon life, I realized I couldn't share it with any of the friends I was so fond of. After seeking help, I began to trust myself more and accept the soul that had resided in me all along. Even though I was happy and proud of my growth, I couldn't share it with the people who were supposed to love me. I had to stay hidden, holding tight to hope and mere memories of friends. Holding tight to a daydream of a sister-life that wasn't meant for me. A sister-life would've required me to find contentment as a submissive and dutiful Mormon woman, surrounded by a community of fellow believers to love me.

As Cheryl Strayed says, "I'll never know, and neither will you, about the life you didn't choose. We'll only know that whatever that sister-life was, it was important and beautiful and not ours. It was the ghost ship that didn't carry us. There's nothing to do but salute it from the shore."

So here I am, saluting it from the shore. Bidding it adieu. And it's painful. Sometimes it still hurts to know that many of my friends and family can only love me on a surface level, because they hold tighter to their religion, indoctrination and belief system.

When someone leaves the church, they don't always want to say goodbye to the people in it. They just want to be loved for who they are, and they want to love others in return—but too often this right is denied. Once a person leaves, there is no more room for love. Both parties feel rejected, hurt and scorned. The post-Mormon is closed out, shunned and only spoken of in gossip groups and rumor mills. The service projects for these people and their families come to an abrupt end. Their children are excluded from neighborhood playdates. Their families stop inviting them to reunions, camping trips and Christmas dinners.

The doors to love that have always been open to them are now only opened on a conditional basis. They can only be unlocked with a magical key—a key of acceptance due to unwavering belief and absolute submission. And if you do not possess one of these magical keys, you are denied unconditional love and acceptance for who you are. But remember, your right as a human is to live your truth and no one has a right to condemn you for living it. It goes both ways.

Respect must be had on both sides.

I will say that something I never considered when I left the church was the potential hurt that I would be causing those I love by leaving. In my mind I was searching for my authentic self. That should make those that love me happy, right? But I discovered that when a person leaves the LDS church, it is almost seen as an act of rejection, which feels extremely personal to the still-believing members. While I never intended to reject them, I understand how that could feel. The Mormon foundation is built on community, and when one person leaves the community it sends shock waves through it. In my attempt to find myself and live authentically, there is a real possibility that my actions left those within the church that I loved feeling like they lost a friend.

That was never my intention.

I will be the first one to tell you that I am not a perfect friend, daughter, wife or mom. When I left, I went into hiding. I refrained from posting too much on social media—God forbid someone see me in a tank top relaxing in the sunshine. I stopped reaching out to my friends—all of whom were Mormon. I adjusted my actions and speech habits around Mormon family members so I wouldn't upset them. Even after leaving, I was still so worried about checking boxes and meeting the expectations and standards of other people that I wasn't living for myself. I was so uncomfortable and scared that I felt hiding my true self was the best option because I couldn't handle the idea of being rejected by the people I loved so much.

I felt this way because the culture of the church does not have room for people like me. People who tried for years to make it work, but ultimately decided staying wasn't best for their mental, emotional or spiritual health. People who felt it was best to start a new chapter elsewhere. When you become one of these people, the culture of the church automatically labels you as apostates, lazy learners, unruly children, bitter fruits and sinners. People who were among God's chosen sons and daughters but let go of the iron rod for worldly happiness and the temptations of Satan. I couldn't face that, so I hid instead, like many of you are or have done. I hid my true self to receive love, respect and to be treated fairly—without being discriminated against.

After years of living this way—and lots of talk therapy— I made a conscious effort to grow into myself so I didn't have to feel this way anymore. I desperately wanted to invite my Mormon friends and loved ones back into my life without hiding who I was. But I first had to learn how to communicate out of love instead of anger. I had to learn to not be defensive or shut down. I had to learn how to set boundaries and accept boundaries from other people respectfully. I also had to learn that if my true self was denied by them, I would have to accept it and move forward with my life without them. If we can't ask them to place conditions on our love, then we can't do that either. Sometimes we can easily get caught in that trap.

As you read this book, my biggest hope for you is that you understand that your truth does not mean you are part of some kind of anti-Mormon or anti-Orthodox agenda. Being open about your life experiences is not hate speech against a church. You own your story, just as I own mine. No one can tell you that your experiences and perceptions and thoughts aren't real. I hope this book entangles your heart strings and forces you to think with an open mind and heart. I hope it helps you accept yourself in all your uniqueness, strength and power. I hope you know without a doubt that you deserve love of the highest degree without religious pretenses attached. I hope you know that you too deserve to have a *Vixen* moment, and you *can* be all...*that*.

Sometimes our souls are so big and powerful that they cannot be contained by religion. Sometimes our purpose is so far reaching that no organization can contain us. Sometimes the Godliest thing to do is to be true to ourselves.

eunice

Somewhere along the way,
I traded my soul for a façade of eternal bliss.

On the day that I had become Eunice I was 19 and about to be married.

Lindsay is my given name, but Eunice was my other name. Not my middle name. Not my nickname. Eunice was the name given to me on the day I went to the temple to receive my endowments, which is a sacred Mormon ceremony laden with symbolism where a person makes covenants with God.

My "new name" was only used once—during the initial endowment ceremony—and was meant to be used again only once, after death in heaven. A spiritual badge of honor, I suppose.

This new name, Eunice, symbolized my coming of age—another step achieved on my path to celestial glory. The box of righteousness checked. A name that my husband would call me forth at heaven's gates if we both had endured faithfully to the end. Eunice is the name I swore to never speak aloud outside of the temple doors. I was told it was so sacred I should never speak it to anyone other than my husband, and even then I should only speak of it inside the temple.

The temple is a place only the most faithful and diligent can go. And for years, I stayed faithful. I wanted more than anything to be worthy of the symbolism behind my name—kind of like a recently promoted general living up to his title. He worked hard for it. He earned it. And now he has to walk the walk and talk the talk. He lives differently because of his title—his new name.

My new name had changed me.

I had checked the proverbial temple-shaped box and there was no going back. I now had the responsibility of forever keeping my contract with God in good standing. Eunice became my secret, sacred title. A pact with God that I would endure to the end. That I could stay valiant enough during my life on earth, that I could be worthy enough to be called by my new name in heaven.

Looking back, the true Lindsay was gone long before Eunice was bestowed upon her. She had been intricately groomed for that day after years of checking boxes to fit the mold of what a "good Mormon girl" should look like. It started at 13 in Young Women when my virtue was compared to a piece of chewed gum. It continued at 14, when I was scolded for holding a boy's hand at the movie theater. It continued at 16 while attending EFY (a teen church camp of sorts) at Brigham Young University-Idaho (BYU-I). I had to bend over in front of my female camp counselor so she could do a modesty check before I could leave the dorm room. And it continued until the day I sat through my third and final worthiness interview, prior to marrying my husband where I was asked in depth questions about my sexual practices.

Long before I suppressed myself into living that way, I was a vibrant knock-your-socks-off kind of child. I had wit and cleverness. I wore a backwards baseball cap and sported a short blonde bob. I ran around the desert behind my grandparents' house all day and returned home smelling like sage and Russian olive trees. The sandy trails were my safe haven. The jack rabbits were my friends. I craved wildness and freedom. My purple bike was my rocket ship to adventure. I was wholly me—never concerned about what my body could do to men or if I was "enough." The rabbits and the desert didn't ask that of me.

By the time I had become Eunice, I was half the girl I used to be—even though I didn't see it at the time. I had traded the desert for a church pew. My backwards baseball cap for a dress and a pair of pantyhose. My cleverness and wit and sense of adventure for rules, scripture memorization and Sunday school.

I traded my wildness for conformity.

Somewhere along the way, the jack rabbits forgot my name. Somewhere along the way, I realized that my wildness did not fit in the box of expectations that were built for me. Somewhere along the way, a muzzle was placed on my womanhood in an effort of submission.

Somewhere along the way, I traded my soul for a façade of eternal bliss.

After I had become Eunice, it was like I blindfolded my soul and had begun to move mechanically in my own body. But I lived up to the image of Eunice. I became a wife long before I was ready. Soon after, I became a mom. I read my scriptures every day and prayed over every meal. I watched wholesome television. I never cursed or drank alcohol or wore shorts above my knees. I served in the women's organization and taught adult Sunday school. I spoke in Sacrament meetings and bore my testimony every chance I could. I handed out the *Book of Mormon* to non-believers. I was a living, breathing poster child of Mormon perfection. Every day was a list of dos and don'ts that promised eternal salvation. A list that I mastered through absolute submission.

And I had hid any semblance of independent thought under the hat of Eunice.

For years my true self, the true Lindsay, had been beating at the locked doors to my soul. Eunice, steadfast and devout, had stood guard ensuring me that if I stayed in my place it would be safer for the both of us. I had screamed and writhed and ached. Like a wild animal forced into captivity, I had fought the cage Eunice had placed me in with a carnal ferocity that even *she* had started to take notice. Even *she* started to get curious.

Then one day, Eunice opened the doors just a crack. Just enough to peek at the wild, unyielding, brave creature that fought inside.

And there was no going back.

genesis

*If these grownups can't love each other,
how can they love me?*

The last thing I had remembered before they knocked me out was screaming. I jumped and writhed on the hospital gurney like a girl fighting for her life. Within seconds the gurney was surrounded by nurses with blurred faces and hands. So many hands—reaching for me all at once. One set belonged to my mom.

She couldn't control me either.

Finally, one of the flailing hands made contact and squeezed hard. This hand was big enough to touch forefinger to thumb around my toothpick-sized arm. A half a second later a sharp prick radiated through my skin, and then I fell into blackness.

My eyes opened hours later. My vision was out of focus and I had felt dizzy. The room was dim and the door leading out was open, and a brightness flowed into the room in a perfect rectangle.

There was a beeping coming from somewhere, and I had wondered why. The sound was oddly familiar—like a microwave beeping. I was concerned that someone's food was done being microwaved and they'd forgotten it. I wondered what they were cooking. I willed myself to wake faster so I could let someone know.

I tried to move but was too weak to move anything other than my eyelids. For a few moments, I stared at the ceiling and focused on the bland speckled tiles above me. I tried to count the black specks, but after a few seconds the specks had blurred together and my eyes closed again.

With my eyes closed, I had begun to move my toes slowly, and then my fingers. But when I got to my right index finger, it felt heavy. Like someone had locked it in one of those Chinese finger traps I used to get at Chuck E. Cheese. I tried to move it again. Whatever it was, was pinching my finger. Hard. I willed my other fingers to investigate. It was heavy and bulky and uncomfortable. I didn't like it.

My other fingers on that hand weren't coordinated enough to slip the bulky object off my finger, so I started moving my other hand. My left hand twitched like a dying animal but it wouldn't lift off the bed. It was like suddenly my tiny body was made of cement. Again, I tried to lift the hand with the heaviness on it. This time I was able to lift it slightly, but not for long, and certainly not up to my face or other hand. So instead, I slid my hand toward my belly. Once it was out from under the blanket, I could see what was causing me to feel the heaviness on my finger. It was a black box stuck on the tip of my index finger.

"What is that?" I had wondered. A few seconds later I slid my left hand up to my belly to meet my right hand. Then I pulled the black box off my finger. Suddenly, the microwave beeping stopped. They must've finally gotten their food, I had thought. But now a loud screeching *BEEP!* replaced the microwave sound.

My mom stood from her chair with her book in hand, startled. Doctors and nurses had come running in and suddenly I was surrounded by a swarm of hands. Again.

Holding the black box in one hand and staring at everyone blankly, the doctor shook his head and forcefully shoved the heavy black box back on my finger. I scowled. The microwave beeping started again.

28

As the medical team filed out of my room one by one, my mom kissed my forehead and whispered, "You have to leave that on," before forcing a smile.

A port had been surgically inserted under my left clavicle. I didn't know it yet but would soon discover that there was more than a black box stuck to my body. A two-foot tube, the diameter of a dime, was also secured to my port. My mom would later secure the tube with a bandage around my chest so I wouldn't drag it around or rip it out while playing. But for now, it laid with me on the bed and spanned almost the entire length of my tiny 4-year-old body.

After being discharged from the hospital, my mom, in-home nurse and grandpa took turns injecting my tube with medicine twice a day.

Back then, I was often ill with sinus infections so severe I was unable to breathe and suffered from migraines. My sinuses and lungs were often full of mucus, leaving me bedridden in pain and my medical team concerned. The port was our last resort. My body wasn't responding to other medication, so they decided to inject it right into my bloodstream using my heart as the pump. They weren't sure if it would work. Lucky for me, it did.

For three months, I wore my tube strapped to my chest with a bandage. During this time, I had started Kindergarten and played just like any other kid. The only constraint put on me was running, which would cause my tube to detach from my port. It was also kind of painful, since the port would move with the motion of my arms. So, it wasn't hard for me to remember to not run. Other than that, I hardly noticed my tube or port at all.

Each morning before I went to school I took my treatment, and each day when I got home I took another. And in a matter of weeks, I went from a pale sickly child to one that was full of color and life. The black circles under my eyes lightened. The pain in my head stopped throbbing. I could actually breathe with my mouth closed for the first time in months.

Shortly before the surgery, my mom and I had moved from the little rambler we shared together to my grandparents' house in the next town over. My mom needed a lot of support during those first years of my life and leaned into her family the best way she knew how. But we ended up living at my grandparent's house longer than my mom had anticipated. Much longer. We moved in when I was 4, and back out when I was 17.

It was just me and her during that time. My parents' relationship didn't work out. A lot of really shitty stuff happened in the first few years of my life. I don't have many specific memories of those times, but I remember anger being present. Grown adults fighting like children. Power struggles. Unfair advantages. Lack of maturity. I've heard both sides and honestly, I think I know the truth but it's painful. For most of my life I grew up hearing two different sides to the same story. Both were at fault. Both contributed to the anger. No one was right in an absolute kind of way. Both were left deeply injured—both left scars that are still healing decades later.

But I have always been loved—deeply. I felt that in my formative years. What I would come to learn a few decades later is that everyone shows love differently. The only reason one kind of love feels better than another is because certain kinds of love speak to each of us. And that special love hits our souls differently.

Each relationship within my family unit is vastly different from one another. During my youth I learned quickly which adults I could trust with my emotions. I learned quickly what each of them expected from me and what I could expect from them. I

30

watched how they treated one another and what the dynamics of their relationships with each other were like.

I grew up around just as much love as there was anger. There was a fine line between being loved and being the source of conflict. And this is why I learned to articulate so well. And that may very well be the reason I became a writer. No one could be angry with me in the pages of my journals or in the private thoughts of my developing brain. It was just me there. But those journals and those thoughts didn't start then—at age 4. What started then was the ability to observe like an eagle, scouting its next meal from a mile away. Instead of searching for food, I was scouting energy, moods, tones and learning to dissect words to detect their true meaning. What started then was the curiosity that, *if these grownups can't love each other, how can they love me?*

The plan wasn't to stay with my grandparents for too long. Certainly not 13 years. My mom just needed help with my medical treatment, which involved having an in-home nurse for a while, until she could train the rest of my family to care for me. My mom was still working full-time at this point and relied on my grandparents, the nurse, my pediatrician and my teachers at my elementary school to assure I was cared for. Then, when my grandpa got cancer, my mom quit her job to run his wine store while he underwent invasive treatments and surgeries.

The months quickly turned into a year. The year turned into another. Then, we lost the wine store and my mom decided to go back to college. So, we decided to stay.

Over time, my frail body grew in strength, and soon I was just like any other kid. I climbed trees and made forts and went exploring through the sandy eastern Washington desert. I played sports, had lemonade stands and loved to get as high as I could on the swings. I felt normal, to an extent. But there was something kids my age weren't too concerned about and I caught on fairly quickly. I remember feeling a pull inside of me to explore something bigger. Something without words, but later I would learn that what I was searching for was my faith.

magic

As my own spirit grew in strength,
I regained my sense of purpose,
power and the realization that I
have magic within me.

When I was 9 years old, I had a premonition. I was sitting in front of my bedroom mirror taking in my appearance and daydreaming about my future. Who would I be when I grew up?

Would I be a scientist? A world traveling photographer? The first female President of the United States?

I wanted answers. I knew I had something big and bold to do with my life, I felt it inside of me—squirming around, like my soul was too big for my young body. I sat there staring, hoping, dreaming.

Then it happened.

The reflection of my face and body and everything transformed inside the mirror. Suddenly I was a woman. My smile was huge, and my eyes were kind but focused and purposeful. I remember thinking I was beautiful, almost like how a young girl looks at a Disney princess or an older sister. The premonition only lasted a split second, but the image of that moment burned inside of my mind and I've never forgotten it.

When I look into the mirror now, at nearly 30 years, I don't have as much excitement. I see my tired eyes set deep inside rings of black. I see adult acne and forehead wrinkles. I see the sagging body of a woman who grew another inside of her. Sometimes I see defeat. Other days I see nothing at all, because I

33

don't even make it that far. And, before I know it, I am tucking my son into bed in the same clothes I slept in the night before without looking into a mirror at all. Sometimes, when I look into the mirror I long to see that little girl staring back at me. I miss having the zest of a young girl dreaming of her future without pause.

The girl that raced homemade wooden hydroplanes behind her bike and charged neighbors five cents to watch the races. The girl that unapologetically shopped in the boy's section because the clothes appealed to her more and fit her better. The girl that earned her black belt in Tae Kwon Do at 13 and passed her test with honors because of her dedication and hard work. The girl that raised money at her lemonade stand for the families affected by 9/11 and donated the entire proceeds to a local charity supporting the cause. The girl that desperately sought something bigger than herself because she knew that knowledge could help her change the world someday.

Sometimes, when life seems especially monotonous and hard, I search for her in the mirror.

I recently watched the movie, *About Time*. It begins with a 21-year-old man learning that he has a gift. A gift that his father, and his father before him, also had. It was the gift of time travel. But there was one downfall to his gift—he could only go backwards into the past, never forwards into the future.

For the first 21 years of his life, he had no inkling that he had magic within him. It wasn't until his father, the most trusted man in this young man's life, shared with him their secret gift. His father had waited until his son's 21st birthday to tell him about his gift because of how powerful it was. He needed to wait until his son was mature enough to handle such magic.

34

One especially hard day, as I stared into the mirror searching for that incredible girl, I found myself putting this story into play in my own life. What magic do I have? If I could time travel, would I want to go back in time? Would I change anything? And I thought to myself, I wouldn't change a thing. Not even the hardest parts. Maybe I would want to go back in time just out of curiosity, but I would be terrified to change anything because today my life is amazing and just how it should be.

I honestly wouldn't change a thing if it meant keeping the life I have now.

But, if I went back, what would I do? Would I talk to her—my younger self? Would I tell her about her magic—her purpose? Would I tell her what she's going to do with her life, or that she would forsake herself in search of the magic that was already within her?

Or would I let her figure it out for herself?

I think I already know the answer, because this fiery brave girl doesn't do a damn thing that anyone tells her to do. While she'd be curious and interested, she's the kind that blazes her own path. And she's the kind that needs the space to figure things out for herself. Even if that means going down the path where she would ultimately forsake herself to find her power. Just like the young man in the movie, I knew this girl would have to live in the dark for a while until she reached a more awakened level of consciousness, higher maturity and greater understanding that could truly welcome her own magic.

First, I had to look for magic elsewhere before I could realize my own inherent magic that I possessed all along. I converted to Mormonism for many reasons, but one of them was to feel a connection to the magic of a celestial force—something I'd always believed in but didn't have much knowledge of.

I'd always known, even as Eunice, that there was something powerful within me—like an intrinsic sense of direction, and that is what kept me moving forward. Even when I felt like I was betraying myself. I yearned for more knowledge. For more connection. For more understanding of my own magic.

The irony of it all is that I was not able to recognize the magic of my power until I felt like I had none.

As I lived and breathed Mormonism, where everything was decided for me and my community was a tight knit bubble of sameness, I felt like I had all the answers, all the knowing, and all the tools to achieve greatness. It's easy to feel comfortable in a bubble. And that's exactly how I felt. There was no uncertainty.

I *would* get married. I *would* have children. I *would* complete my "checklist of righteousness." I *would* endure to the end. I *would* be with my family forever in the celestial kingdom. There was no question about it.

It was that plain and simple.

Cults and high control religion feast on the souls of us who are so self-critical and starving for a deeper knowing that we can't see our own power, so we unknowingly give it away to them. And slowly over time our shackles are welded, link by link by the very organizations that claim to free us from our sins—from ourselves.

And so, we become prisoners. We believe we have no power. We turn to them to help us find our way but are always given the same checklists to go over until we start to believe that we just aren't good enough and never will be. If the checklist doesn't work on us, it must be us that's the problem, right? This thought trap quickly leads to cycles of self-blame and self-doubt and lack of self-trust. This is how we lose our power, our magic, and our sense of purpose.

I think stepping into our own power is a journey. Like walking through a tunnel and knowing there is light on the other side, but you have no idea how long the journey will take to get there. The tunnel could take you a few days to pass through, or a lifetime. Along the way, you trip over some rocks, scratch yourself up and move at a slower pace. Other days, you are sprinting towards the light so fast you feel like nothing can stop you. Some days you look back at the path you've come through and think, how much longer? Is it really worth it? Should I just go back?

I often think back to the days of Eunice. I find that those memories come back to me as seen through a veil. Eunice was a dedicated temple-goer. Whenever she needed to "be better" as she wrote in her journals, she would spend hours at the temple, covered head to toe in white with her face veiled, submitting herself to the will of God and silencing the hot-blooded spirit within her.

That is how she tamed that 9-year-old girl's magic—her magic. She tamed it because she was scared of it. Terrified of it. It told her to betray the one thing she perceived gave her all her knowing, all her answers, all her greatness—the church. But eventually, she would find out that her magic did not exist in the temples or the church pews—her magic lay deep, shackled, tormented, veiled.

Eunice squished and squeezed and stretched and fit herself into a new world. One that supposedly had all the answers. One that had a strategic plan to exaltation. And her inner child, that determined girl, wanted to know all the answers because only then could she truly make a difference and help people.

When I let Eunice die, it was almost like I was coming back to myself—to the little girl inside of me with such spark and hope. The minute I let Eunice die, I started sprinting through the tunnel towards my power. The power I had felt as a child. The power I always knew existed. The magic that only I have because there is only one me. Eunice's death was both a spiritual death and a spiritual rebirth. The shackles of conformity slowly fell off as she slowly died. As my own spirit grew in strength, I regained my sense of purpose, power and the realization that I have magic within me.

The beauty in becoming unbound and free, and discovering who you are is that your magic and your purpose also become unbound and free—finally able to reveal themselves. It has always been there, but you just couldn't tap into it. Not until, just like the man in the movie, you reached a point of consciousness and maturity that will leave you capable to handle such power.

And just like Eunice, who had to live in the dark in search of all the answers, until she realized she already had them within herself. Until she reached enlightenment and set her soul free.

Sometimes, that means forsaking your past self that squished and squeezed into a fabricated idea of who you thought you should be, to honor who your soul already is. To honor who your soul always has been.

To honor your magic.

like a lady

*I should've known then that I was never meant
to conform to someone else's expectations.*

I had begun attending The Church of The Nazarene with my friend
Tanya and her family off and on for the first few years of my life.
It would be the only church I attended prior to joining the LDS
church.

One spring when I was 10, it was announced that they
were holding an overnight church camp. Tanya and I thought it
would be fun so we asked our parents if we could go. A few weeks
later, Tanya and I had piled into the church van with our overnight
bags and away we went.

Our first night there we received our cabin assignments
and bunk mates. Tanya and I had never been on a trip away from
home, so we made sure to have our parents request we stay
together.

We arrived in the late afternoon to a camp out in the
woods. Tanya and I grabbed our stuff out of the van and shuffled
into the cultural hall where we waited for our counselor. While we
waited a band played Christian rock music that everyone seemed
to know the words to, except me.

Moments later, a plump woman with a megaphone
screeched through the praising of Jesus to call forward the next
group of girls to receive their cabin assignments. Tanya and I were
called together so we followed the plump woman in a single file

line back to a little cabin. When we arrived, some girls were already there.

"Lindsay," the plump woman said, "you're up there on bunk four. Tanya, you're over here on the bottom of bunk two." Tanya and I looked at each other quizzically. We wanted to be bunkmates too, but it didn't look like that would happen. We shrugged, happy to at least be in the same cabin.

I climbed the ladder to my bunk and was met with a rubber mattress cover. I poked it and it made a scrunching sound beneath my finger. I rolled my sleeping bag out and placed my pillow at the head of my bunk. Then I sat there, unsure of what to do next. I decided to take in my surroundings a bit, but when I did I locked eyes with the girl across from me who was also sitting on her top bunk. She was staring at me.

"Hi," I said quietly, smiling.

"Hi," she replied, not smiling.

"What's your name?" I asked, trying to be friendly.

"Rebecca." she said blankly. I shifted awkwardly on the couch.

"It's nice to meet you," I smiled again. Rebecca said nothing and looked away.

I looked around the cabin, which was made of four sets of wooden bunkbeds with just enough room between them for overnight bags. The bunks were arranged in a way that made one hallway down the middle of the cabin.

Moments later, the plump woman returned without her megaphone and said it was time for dinner. We needed to leave for the mess hall in five minutes.

I climbed down from my bunk and put on a sweatshirt. My friend Tanya sat on her bed with her long legs crisscrossed. I made eye contact with her and could tell both of us were feeling a little awkward and very nervous. I was just about to walk across the cabin to her when a door swung open violently. Out of the door came a young woman fully nude and fully developed. She stared me straight in the eye, flung her towel over her shoulder, and pranced out of the bathroom like a naked show pony.

"Hi," she said with attitude. "I'm Stacy!" She proceeded to prance through the entire cabin bare naked at a solid pace. "By the way, I'm the oldest one here. I'm 13," she swaggered.

I had never seen anyone else's naked body besides my mom's so I looked directly at the floor and stood frozen. As Stacy finished her loop around the cabin, the plump woman returned. She opened the front door to the cabin and her eyes bulged out of her head like a cartoon character.

"Oh, my heavens!" she shouted. "Put your clothes back on, right now!"

I immediately sat down exactly where I was and pulled my knees to my chest. I didn't want to move for fear that I may run into the naked girl in this tight space. Instead of putting her clothes back on, Stacy decided to start sprinting through the cabin, weaving in and out of the bunks and down the main walkway... still naked except now she was whipping her towel erratically through the air.

"You can't tell me what to do!" Stacy screamed.

The plump woman immediately put out an SOS on her walkie talkie and told us to leave the cabin and wait for her on the porch outside. All of us filed out of the cabin while Stacy continued her wild protest. It took three camp counselors to wrangle Stacy into some clothes.

We were the last cabin to arrive in the mess hall that day. My belly rumbled. I hadn't eaten since breakfast. If Stacy had to cause a naked fuss, why did it have to be at dinner time?

When we were finally able to dish up at the buffet, I was excited to discover that cheeseburgers were on the menu that evening. I loaded my burger with bacon, lettuce and tomato. I asked for two scoops of fries and got extra ketchup and mayo to make fry sauce. I hurried back to our table with Tanya in tow. Excitedly, we both picked up our burgers and took the biggest bites we could. We looked at each other and said "mmm" in unison, then giggled while the juice dripped from our chins.

"Excuse me ladies!" a loud voice bellowed from behind us. "Elbows off the table! And take smaller bites! It's not polite to have your mouth full like that!"

Tanya and I looked at each other with surprise. Still holding my burger, I lifted my elbows two inches off the table and held them there.

"How are we supposed to eat a burger without our elbows on the table?" I leaned over to Tanya and asked.

She shrugged.

I continued eating until the plump woman returned and was scolded again for my elbows being back on the table.

"Let's have a lesson on how to eat a cheeseburger like a lady, shall we?" she asked, but didn't wait for our answer before continuing. "First, place your napkin on your lap. Pick up your burger with both hands and take a small bite. *Do not* put your elbows on the table. Now, while you're chewing, place your burger back on your plate and sit up straight. Wipe your mouth and take a drink if you must."

I sat there staring at my cheeseburger with the most disgusted look on my face. I'd never wanted to punch a person so badly in the 10 years I'd been alive. I felt like I went into some kind of time warp back to the 50s. My belly gargled in protest, but I did the only thing I could do. I bit my tongue, put my napkin on my lap, and followed the plump woman's instructions of how to eat a burger like a lady. After each bite, I wiped my mouth gently and took a sip of water.

When I was done eating, I willed my mind back to the smell of Russian olive trees after a fresh summer rain and the feeling of rough bark on my skin. The cooing of mourning doves that sung to me each day outside my window. My grandma's kitchen table where I could eat a cheeseburger how I wanted. I closed my eyes for a moment to take it all in. I almost believed I was back home when one of my cabinmates ran out of the bathroom screaming.

"Rebecca is puking in the bathroom!" she yelled. The mess hall went silent. The plump woman rushed away from our table and into the bathroom. She was gone for what seemed like an hour. All of us sat there at our table, while the others slowly made their way to evening activities.

We would later learn that Rebecca was bulimic.

"What does that mean?" I had asked innocently.

"It means she makes herself puke every time she eats!" Stacy snapped from across the table.

"Oh," I said.

I wondered why anyone would want to do that and how they could. I hadn't really thrown up that much as a child, but the times I did I remember it feeling terrible. I couldn't understand *why* someone would want to make themselves feel that way.

That night, as I laid directly across from Rebecca, I watched her sleep. Her shoulders moved heavily with each breath she took. She was a bigger girl and I wondered if that was why she made herself throw up. I wondered if her mom knew about what she did. I wondered why she was so sad. I wondered if she was embarrassed that everyone knew her secret now.

I barely slept that night. And in the morning I felt a heavy pit in my stomach, like I'd swallowed a boulder. I didn't like this place. I didn't like these people. I didn't like eating a cheeseburger like a lady. I didn't like naked Stacy. I didn't like any of it. When the plump woman arrived to take us to our morning activities, a feeling of dread came over me.

"Good morning, ladies!" she had chirped. "We have quite the day planned for you today! First, we will head to breakfast in the mess hall, then we have our Manners Course and after that you may go swimming in the lake until lunch! Remember, one-pieces only—I don't want to see any tummies!"

I had wondered briefly what a "Manners Course" was, and then my rumbling belly told me to forget about it and go directly towards the food. We ate breakfast and, sure enough, Rebecca threw up again. The plump woman sat staring at her plate with her napkin on her lap and gave a heavy sigh. Afterwards, we cleaned our table and headed to the Manners Course in another building within the camp.

The second I stepped in the door I wanted to bolt back out. Inside the room was a large ten-person table perfectly set in a semi-formal manner. On the opposite side of the room was a desk with a phone and notepad. Adjacent to the desk was a stack of books on a shelf with a line of masking tape on the floor. The Manners Course instructor told us to sit at the table.

"Hello, and welcome to the Manners Course!" she said after we were all seated. "Today we will be breaking into groups of three, and each group will complete each of the three stations. Station one is table setting, station two is phone etiquette, and station three is book balancing for proper posture. Let's get started!"

For the next few hours, I learned how to properly set a table, how to properly answer a phone, and how to walk, properly of course. And of *course*, I found a way to make the unbearable bearable.

To the dismay of the instructor, I was very good at balancing a book on my head and grew bored of that station almost immediately—so I challenged the other girls to a "proper" book balancing race. As you can imagine, it escalated quickly. What once was a room filled with only the sounds of clanking silverware and overly polite conversation had grown loud with the giggles of girls running like racing robots around the room—their books quickly falling to the floor with a clash. It was the most fun anyone had had since naked Stacy had taken her prance about the cabin the day before.

The rest of my time there is a bit of a blur, I never slept well and Rebecca continued to throw up after every meal. Stacy scared the living hell out of me. The worship music was weird, and people waved their hands in the air and cried because they loved Jesus so much. I didn't get it. And as much as I had wanted to find my faith, that was not it.

After three days, I called my mom and told her I wanted to come home. I just couldn't take it anymore. Tanya's dad picked us up the next day.

I should've known then that I was never meant to conform to someone else's expectations. That God didn't make me "proper." That no matter how far away I traveled from the desert, the wildness of it was still within me—calling me, showing me the way. I should've known then that my wildness was never meant to be tamed.

I continued to attend that church on and off for a couple more years until I stopped altogether. While I liked feeling like a part of a church community and I liked going with Tanya, I never felt my wildness there. Instead I had felt stifled but still had a deep, unquenchable yearning to know more about God.

I didn't know it then, but a shift was coming. A pre-ordained bigger-than-me kind of shift. A shift that determined the rest of my life. I didn't find my faith there, at that camp or at that church. But it came, because the pull I'd felt was toward my destiny. However, my life had to change altogether before that would happen. First, someone and something had to come into my life... and tilt my world on its axis.

the choice

The church became my burning phoenix.
My symbol of hope.

By the time I was 11, we'd lived with my grandparents for roughly seven years and my mom was dedicated to finishing her bachelor's degree. I had watched her struggle, and I struggled with understanding why she'd want to go to college if it meant not having her own house or her own life.

"Your education is the one thing no one can ever take from you," she'd say to me.

I didn't get it.

Around that time, my mom had started dating the man who would later become my stepdad—someone I grew to love deeply. But at a young age, I went through extreme, life-altering changes. Ones that I wouldn't be able to make sense of until I grew into adulthood and became a parent myself. Ones that, even now, I am exploring tirelessly.

It all started with a knock on the door.

It was dark outside and my grandparents had already gone to bed—each asleep in their separate quarters of the house. But my mom and I had often stayed up to watch our favorite shows, snuggled in her bed. We'd rotate between *Unsolved Mysteries* and *LOST*. On the nights that *LOST* was on she'd let me stay up an extra half hour past my bedtime, just so we could watch it together and gush at the mystery of it all. The next day, we'd discuss our theories on where we believed the storyline was headed.

That night, the heavy knock on the door had caught us by surprise. And when I answered it, our lives changed.

There, standing on the front steps was a tall, good-looking man about the same age as my mom. His hair was buzzed and dark brown. His goatee was well trimmed, surrounded by a five o'clock shadow. I could tell from his clothes that he worked in construction—Carharts, He was wearing Romeos and had paint-stained hands.

"Hi, is Kelly home?" he had asked.

I looked at him quizzically, I had never opened the door to find a man asking for my mom.

"Um, yes. Hold on a sec," I said.

Without thinking, I shut the door, leaving him out on the front porch. I ran up the stairs of our split-level home and remembered I needed to tread lightly because my grandpa was sleeping in the basement below. I tiptoed quickly through the hall to find her.

"Mom, there's a guy at the door for you." My mom furrowed her brow in response. She seemed as confused as I was.

"Who is it?" she asked.

"I dunno!" I said as I hopped back onto her bed. "He just asked if you were home and I said yes!"

"You just left him out there?"

"Well yeah… I don't know him!" She sighed and walked out of the bedroom.

I trailed close behind her, but instead of going down the stairs to the door, I sat on the adjacent stairs that lead up to the third story loft—the perfect spy location. I could hear everything, but they couldn't see me. As she walked down the stairs she tilted her head in an attempt to see through the windows who the strange man was on the other side of the front door. It wasn't until she got to the door that she recognized him. She opened the door and shrieked.

"Oh my God! Kenny! What are you doing here? Come inside!" They hugged and she welcomed him into our home.

My heart sank. I think, even at that age, I knew what journey was ahead. I couldn't verbalize it, but my intuition knew that my mom's love was about to be spread a little thinner. I knew this new person would change my young life.

Never before had I needed to compete for her love and affection, and my initial knee-jerk reaction had been one of hostility. I never had to share my mom's attention. And because of the uncertainty of the relationships around me, I had felt guarded. From a young age, my mom had been my person. The only one who prioritized me. The only one who had given me the kind of love my soul had needed. Was I going to be alone if someone else joined our lives? Could she love more than one person? Was there room for all of us? I was apprehensive. I was scared. All of this was foreign to me, and I didn't have the capacity or maturity to understand it.

It had been a long journey that began that night. But eventually, that strange man on the porch became my mom's boyfriend. They had reconnected that night, after years apart. I didn't realize it until many, many years later, but Kenny returning to my mom's life was part of a bigger plan. A plan that not only involved my destiny, but the destiny of my future husband, our lineage and about half a dozen other people.

My entire future had tilted on its axis that day.

As their relationship continued to grow and they eventually married, I had begun to feel emotions I couldn't make sense of. Waves of anger, confusion, jealousy, fear, and what I know now to be grief.

And my grief was complicated—especially as a young teen. Typically, new relationships wouldn't have sparked this kind of emotion in me, yet there I was grieving and didn't know it. Looking back now, I think I was grieving the end of the two-of-us-against-the-world bond we had. I was grieving a change I didn't see coming—a change I hadn't been prepared for.

My mom had always been, and still is, my rock. We've been partners in crime since the womb. People have often described us as the real-life Gilmore Girls. The Lorelei and Rory of dusty eastern Washington. We did everything together. But when Kenny knocked on the door that night, that changed. A new person came into our world that I wasn't used to, nor was I ready for it. Kenny took me by surprise. Then, eventually, his two girls came into our lives as well. We had gone from a two-woman girl gang to a party of five seemingly overnight. And at that same time, I was undergoing the change of puberty, graduating to high school, figuring out where I fit in and where I didn't, as well as a transition out of martial arts—which I had been doing daily for the last three years.

My young world had been the heaviest thing I had ever carried on my shoulders. I felt a great deal of stress at that time but couldn't always verbalize it very well. Instead, I was just grumpy. All the time. I wanted my mom to be happy, but I didn't know how to be a daughter to anyone else. I didn't know how to be a sister to someone. I didn't know how to watch my mom love someone else—anyone else. I didn't know how to react when the world wasn't just about me, about us anymore.

During the earliest years of my life, change had always been negative. When my mom and I had moved into our little rambler, it was because my parents broke up. When we moved into my grandparents' house, it was because I was sick. When my mom changed jobs, it was because my grandpa had cancer. Change made me nervous, unsure, and filled with anxiety. Additionally, I was terrified of being left behind. Forgotten about.

When my parents broke up, there was a lot of anger involved and I had felt left behind. Even though everyone involved was fighting *for* me, at some point, it became a power struggle—and I wondered how much of that was really about me and how much of it was really the battle of the alpha. It was so bad that I didn't know anyone in my dad's family until adolescence, and I am still working on these relationships today.

Because of all of the fighting, blaming, lying and anger, I had felt that one wrong step would cause me to be left again. Like if that fine line between love and contention were crossed, I'd be on the outs.

And then, there was this new person. This new family had come into my life with a completely different dynamic, and I had been worried that my mom liked them more. That my mom who had struggled for so long had seen a better and easier life with them, and I would be left behind or forced into a new life that felt like abandonment—the abandonment of our old life, of our old relationship for something new. As an adult, I can see clearly how this was affecting me—but at the time, I couldn't comprehend it all.

My way of dealing with this inner panic was to seek affirmation in other places. It had become my safety net. Like if I got left behind I had a backup plan, because if I ever lost my mom I knew I wouldn't be okay. I was smart and grounded enough to know where not to look for affirmation, but I had still needed it desperately. I started looking for positive affirmation from people at school. When I didn't receive it, I expanded my circle and began to seek new friendships. I may not have known how to be a sister to someone, but I knew how to be a friend. So that had become my M.O.

Then one day, I met the Mormon kids and they were amazing. They had welcomed me with open arms like I'd never experienced. They were kind and fun and goofy like I was. They were also interested in topics like faith, God, a greater purpose, and doing good in the world. Many of them were more mature, in this aspect, than those of their non-LDS peers. I had felt a connection to them, like I was finally understood. Their culture was professional in building community, and this was showcased by how well their youth came together.

I had never experienced this level of community before. It was chaotic love. Each of them had at least four siblings, and the girl who became my best friend came from a family of 12 children. It blew my mind. And they all knew each other—all of them. Each Mormon family knew the other Mormon families because they went to the same church, and their friendships extended outside the church walls.

As my friendships with the Mormon kids grew, I had begun to hang out at their houses, and they had always been messy and crazy with tons of people everywhere. I loved it. It was so different than the quiet, clean, immaculate home I shared with my grandparents. They fought with their siblings like rabid animals and minutes later asked for a ride to the store like nothing happened.

I had begun to attend Mutual, a kind of weekly youth group, on Wednesday nights. The young women and young men met separately three out of the four Wednesdays each month, then on the last Wednesday of the month they had a combined activity.

At this stage of my life, I most loved the traditional aspect of it all. I loved that I was learning how to sew and do service projects. I loved feeling a sense of purpose. Being around these kids had reignited my curiosity around God and faith. I loved feeling special and believing that I could use my special gifts to make the world a better place. The church had become a platform for me to do good things, which fueled me even further. I knew I was created to do good things, to change the world, to connect with other people. The church had provided all of this to me.

It also provided a more traditional family structure. The dynamic of my friends' homes reminded me of "Leave It to Beaver," where moms stayed home and dads worked. And just like the television show, their worlds had been cast in black and white—it had seemed so simple. So easy. They had a mom and dad and siblings—and each of them had a role to play, a chore to do, a manner in which they supported the family unit. It had structure.

It interested me to visit these traditional Mormon homes. I belonged to a home made up of three generations, and my mom was not the head of our household—my grandparents were. And depending on the day, the hat of chief changed chaotically, and was sometimes quarreled over. My grandparents slept in separate bedrooms in separate areas of the house. For the most part, they lived separate lives.

My mom and I shared a room—shared a bed for most of my childhood because I was too scared to be alone. Eventually, we made the room next to hers into a private space for a growing girl. It had become my safe haven. My mom pursued her education in the hopes of getting a higher paying job and moving us into our own home but she juggled being a single mom, helping my grandparents, and pulling her weight to earn our keep in the house. The roles in my home looked very different than those of a traditional Mormon family—than most families at the time.

The LDS belief of an eternal family was a hook, line and sinker for me. It had made me feel for the first time that I would never lose another person I loved. Because in the church you can be sealed together forever.

And that had become my goal.

To be righteous enough that I could be sealed to someone who would love me and never leave me. To bring these teachings home to my mom and she'd want to join the church so we could be sealed, and she would never leave me. We'd be stuck together—no matter what. I'd never lose her, not even in death. Like somehow, this invisible celestial thread would tie us together, and the sense of grief and loss I felt over having new people in our family wouldn't feel so scary. Like maybe, I could accept them and love them fully because I knew that I could never lose my mom… and if I loved them enough, and they loved me enough, I couldn't lose them either.

And maybe, If I joined the church and did enough good things, no one would find enough fault with me to ever leave me. Not my friends, not my family, not my future spouse—not anyone. I would be exalted into this realm of unachievable perfection that would leave me loved by all, and no one would ever leave me again.

I know now that was impossible. I know now this it was unattainable. I know now how ignorant and naive that frame of thinking is because I would later learn that people will always come and go—and sometimes it had nothing to do with me, but within this frame of thinking it *always* had to do with me. It was because I wasn't good enough or I wasn't worth it. And because I had a deep-rooted fear of abandonment that went all the way back to infancy.

So, I became Eunice. What started as a search for validation, a search for purpose, a search for my own faith, and a search for a plan B—just in case I lost my mom, led me toward Mormonism. Toward a rigid religious structure with all the answers—that cast me into a world of black and white where everything was easy and scripted and everyone just knew all the things.

The church became my burning phoenix. My symbol of hope. My chance at rebirth. An opportunity for familial solitude. That someday, through practicing enough faith and good works, I could have the kind of family structure I'd always wanted. One that was more traditional, where people were unified in their cause and there was a mom and a dad that loved each other. Where dads loved their kids more than themselves—so much so that they stay. Where people talked and loved and laughed and hugged more than they fought. Where the line between being loved and contention wasn't so thin. A family where truth and lies did not have to be dissected on a regular basis. A family where love is not withheld as a form of punishment. A family where no one leaves anyone behind.

In my then 13-year-old eyes, the Church of Jesus Christ of Latter-Day Saints embodied all of this for me. It had given me a clear path toward true joy. It had given me friends, good morals and high standards. It had given me peace that I was actively pursuing goodness and becoming a better person each day. It had given me hope that I could have the kind of home I didn't have then.

I had just wanted to belong. I had just wanted to stop being scared that I would be abandoned. And I had wanted it so badly that I was willing to do anything to get it. And all of that wanting came at a cost.

One thing that Eunice and the soul she caged had in common was tenacity. When we wanted something, we went after it until we got it. Nothing could stop us.

Nothing.

Not the wild soul of a desert-kissed girl. Not the memory of her beating heart as she watched her bold, brave mom become *Vixen*. Not the rebellious voice that told her to eat with her elbows on the table. Not even her purple bike, her rocket ship to adventure, could save her now. The table had been set. The napkin was on her lap. She had raised her elbows and taken a bite.

It was done.

dilated

I was taught that sex
was something to be sorry for.

I often look back to the day Travis proposed on bended knee. Just moments before, we had pretended to be Jack and Rose from *Titanic* by reenacting our favorite scene from the movie and spitting off the bridge into the icy water of the Snake River below.

"I can spit like a man!" I had shouted in a thick southern drawl.

We had found that bridge a few months before. The historic foot bridge in eastern Idaho was used during the early settlement of the area. Originally, it was a toll bridge used primarily by farmers and tradesman taking livestock and other necessities across the river to neighboring communities. Decades later, a Chinese garden was built beneath it. Travis and I had been intrigued by it and found it to be so beautiful. The fact that we were there, having a moment together, had made me smile.

As Travis talked, my breath billowed up like clouds from my heaving chest. I heard words coming out of his mouth but couldn't focus long enough to comprehend it all. I caught the fragments of his words, like pieces of confetti falling from the sky.

Love. Forever. Grateful. Life. Happy.

I started to laugh nervously, excitedly. His smile widened and he opened the velvet box. Diamonds set in brilliant white gold glistened like fresh snowflakes. It was then that I realized he'd bought the ring we'd looked at a few weeks prior. The ring both of us had fallen in love with.

Finally, with a trembling voice Travis asked, "Lindsay, will you marry me?"

I laughed loudly and shouted, "Yes!" He slid the ring onto my finger. It was a perfect fit. Travis stood and pulled me into him, kissing me as we both giggled with excitement.

As undergraduate college students at BYU-I, this kind of quick courtship was normal. In fact, we had many friends who met and married within only a matter of a few weeks. A four-month courtship was actually quite long in some instances. And on top of that, we had decided to wait another six months to marry so we could have a summer wedding. This had made our courtship 10 months, which is almost unheard of in the Mormon community. This is mostly due to the fact that to be married and sealed in the temple, both parties must be living the law of chastity—no sex, no necking, no touching.

Nothing.

Waiting almost a year to be physically intimate in any kind of way was a very, very, *very* long time. But in order to stay in school we had to adhere to the strict "no premarital sex" policy.

There were safeguards put in place at BYU-I to ensure this policy was being followed. We had curfews which were strictly enforced, and all of us were taught to be "our brothers' keepers." If we saw our roommates sneaking in after curfew often, we were to report it to the student honor code office. Additionally, Travis wasn't allowed in my room—technically he wasn't even allowed to use my bathroom, but none of us followed that rule. All student-approved housing was built in a manner that had an open concept living area and kitchen with a hallway leading back to the bathrooms and bedrooms. A door was attached to the entryway of the hall signaling the "no-go" zone for the opposite sex. If males were seen frequenting the bedrooms in a female's apartment, the student honor code office would take action and an investigation would take place. Any sexual misconduct was grounds for suspension and even expulsion.

The only time Travis and I could be physically affectionate was in a parked car—and even there the church had a firm grip on us. We were never truly alone. Even in our private affections, the church was a prominent, booming voice in our heads—the only true voice in our consciousness.

As our wedding day approached, my roommate had asked if I had made a "pre-marital appointment."

Confused I asked, "What's a pre-marital appointment?"

"You haven't heard of a pre-marital appointment?" she had squealed. "All the girls here do it. It's like a check-up but they prepare you for your wedding night."

In Mormonism, sex is a like a Christmas gift that you open at the right time, on the right day, with the right person. The thought of preparing for it was like the surprise Christmas Eve present no one told you was coming.

"Oh, okay. Well, that sounds good," I said. "I should probably do it because I've never even been to a gynecologist before." And so, I made the appointment like a giddy schoolgirl.

Days later, I was in the exam room, legs spread open like a turkey at Thanksgiving dinner. I had requested a female doctor and was happy they had someone available. I had felt anxious, like I swallowed a rock. No one had ever seen my naked body before and now this woman was going to give me an uncomfortable exam. I had a general idea of what was going to happen for the pap smear, my mom and I had talked about it a couple of years before. What I was unsure of was... everything else. What made *this* appointment any different than just a check-up? What made *this* appointment a "pre-marital exam?"

The doctor inserted what I envision to be a very long Q-tip, and I winced. It felt weird, like someone had scratched me from the inside.

"Can you scoot down further on the table please?" she asked as she momentarily poked her head up from my nether regions, before sinking back down into the abyss. My vagina was gaping open like one of those plants that eats bugs, and her arm was the fly. I scooted, I jiggled, and I wondered what my vagina looked like as it paraded itself down to the edge of the table. I was so embarrassed. I hated the feeling of someone that close to my naked and exposed body.

The doctor continued conversation like it was nothing, but I couldn't muster a word. She kept asking me to open my legs wider, and every few seconds I subconsciously closed them again. I didn't want to talk. I didn't want to be there. I didn't know how to respond to someone seeing my nakedness.

It felt wrong.

I felt wrong.

After she was done, she asked me to get dressed and said that she would come back in to chat. I laid there for a moment, staring at the speckled ceiling tiles, thinking about how that was the first time anyone had ever seen my 19-year-old virgin vagina. Briefly, I wondered how other women experienced this kind of appointment and if I should talk to someone, so I didn't feel so alone and awkward.

Thankful to be done, I dressed quickly and folded the gown before neatly laying it on the chair—apologetically, like sorry about my vagina, the least I can do is fold this gown nicely for you.

I returned to the examination table, the paper crunching beneath my weight. The comfort of my clothing was a welcome feeling but I was still reeling from the awkwardness of it all. I pulled my legs to my chest and wrapped my arms around them, holding my body tight.

The doctor knocked and smiled as she walked back into the exam room. I slowly released my legs and feigned some kind of normal posture. How was one supposed to sit after this kind of exam? I decided to sit like the Queen. Knees together, ankles crossed, back straight, hands clasped on my lap, smile plastered on my face. If it worked for the Queen over the last few centuries, I had guessed it would work for me too.

"Okay, Lindsay," she started, "so you've told me that you're getting married soon and you have never had sexual intercourse, correct?"

"Correct," I responded.

"So, do you have any questions or concerns about your wedding night?"

"Um... no," I lied. "I don't think so."

"Okay," she smiled kindly. "Well, everything looked normal and healthy. We will have the results of your pap smear in a few days. They will let you know if anything comes back abnormal. But as far as your wedding night goes, there are some things I am going to send you home with to make it... easier and more comfortable for you."

She walked across the room and opened the cupboard above the sink. I shifted my weight and heard the paper beneath me rip. The familiar crinkling of plastic filled the room. The doctor pulled down a clear plastic bag with what looked like a brochure and some other objects before she sat back down on her stool and wheeled close to me.

"So, this bag has some pamphlets with information about birth control and common questions about your reproductive health. And these," she said as she had pointed to three hard plastic objects, "these are plastic dilators that you will insert into your vagina once a day for a few minutes. There are three different sizes here. Start with the smallest one, which is about the size of a tampon, and move up as you feel comfortable. The larger you go, the more it will be uncomfortable—just at first. These will prepare you for your first-time having intercourse."

Wide-eyed, I smiled awkwardly. I was excited to experience sex for the first time and was curious about the dilators. I had friends in the church that hadn't been allowed to use tampons until after they were married, so the idea that I was encouraged to put something inside of me that would prepare my body for sex had felt a bit exhilarating. It had made me feel like a woman—not just the girl I'd been all my life.

To think I was finally at this huge milestone in my life— my first sexual encounter, it had been something so unknown, but exciting. I had thought this kind of preparation was normal. In my small, controlled world I had been under the impression that every woman did this. I thought every woman needed to prepare herself for her wedding night this way. I thought every woman prepared for sex this way. I thought I was setting myself up for success— preparing my body for something new. I thought that if I didn't do it, I would be in pain and not be able to continue, leading me to disappoint my husband. My more *experienced* husband. Which was already something that had been weighing heavily on me.

"Do you have any questions?" she asked.

"Umm… no. I don't think so."

"Great! Let me know if you need anything. Nice to meet you, Lindsay!"

"Thank you," I said as I uncrossed my ankles and stepped off the examination table.

"Oh! One more thing," she said, coming back into the room. "I am writing you a prescription for an antibiotic. There is a good chance you will get a urinary tract infection your first time and they are no fun! Trust me," she laughed. "So as a precaution, fill this prescription and always remember to pee after sex!"

Dilators. Antibiotics. Pee after sex.

Got it.

I drove back to my apartment, dilators and antibiotics in hand, and had felt proud of my little first-timer sex kit. I felt like a real-life woman. I later told my roommates about them and they asked lots of questions. All of us Mormon virgins giggled with youthful innocence at the thought of preparing for this next step of life. For our rite of passage. For becoming a woman by preparing our bodies for another.

It's been 10 years since that day, the day of my first gynecology appointment. The day I innocently attempted to do what I thought was right. The day that I, yet again, found myself blindly following without question. I did as I was told. And every day for weeks, I wore plastic vaginal dilators as I folded laundry, studied for exams, and did homework.

These "pre-marital exams" where they dole out dilators like candy on Halloween were just another part of the toxic purity culture that is widely accepted and never questioned. I never thought back then to question this practice because with my conditioning it made sense. In my mind I was being responsible, I was preparing my body for another. Because honestly this concept is something I had been taught since the age of 13. My body was to be used to make life. It was desired by men and had the ability to multiply and replenish the earth, just like God commanded.

When it came to sex, I was never taught to say no because I was uncomfortable, I was taught to say no to keep *men* righteous. I was never taught to say yes because I wanted it. I was taught to say yes because it was a commandment within the confines of marriage. So, in my mind I was helping myself because I was scared and unsure, and this helped me feel like I had some kind of control over what was about to happen on my wedding night.

All these years later I think about what I would've done if I had a daughter and she had to experience such an appointment, where she is given dilators that traumatize her virgin body as she prepares herself for a man. Where she feels so much loss of control over her own body that it terrifies her. Where she holds a core belief that her body is not her own, and instead of practicing healthy communication and sexual discovery practices with her partner she relies on the cold, hard, lifeless assistance of a plastic object to prepare herself mentally and physically for what's to come. I think of her, my imaginary daughter, and how she might be experiencing feelings of losing control over her body, and to find that control she gladly accepts this practice to prepare herself for what she's been taught was a sin next to murder outside of marriage.

I still grieve for my young 19-year-old self. My heart aches for her. For years, she had been conditioned to believe that her body was sinful, her nakedness was lustful, and her sexual organs had one purpose. I wish I could go back so I could tell her to walk right out of that place and take control of her sexuality and her body. I would tell her to talk to her fiancé and decide together what makes them happy and comfortable.

But the fact is that Travis and my physical relationship was never allowed to be ours. From our first kiss under the stars in an Idaho potato field until our wedding day, our sexual relationship was decided by the higher powers at hand. And even then, in our bedroom, the church had jurisdiction. The LDS church heavily discourages any kind of sexual conduct that is not conducive to creating life. Our garments were never allowed to touch the floor. Sexual exploration was limited. After Travis and I were married, I was so confused and scared of sex.

And the shame I had been conditioned with didn't magically go away just because I was married either. Suddenly, there was this spiritual aspect to sex that made me feel like I wasn't doing it right. Women in my ward talked about how they would pray before sex or how on their wedding night they read their patriarchal blessings to one another before they became intimate. They spoke in high regard to how they invited God to be the third person in their marriage and it didn't exclude the bedroom. So now there was this new expectation of me that, again, I was not prepared for. Not only was I going through what I know now as religious abuse and trauma from the deep level of conditioning, but I also wasn't living up to the expectation of having "celestial sex."

Travis and I didn't have "celestial sex." We didn't pray before or afterwards. Our garments touched the floor. We used condoms and birth control. Eventually we started to experiment with oral sex and toys. And instead of feeling normal, I had felt both ashamed and liberated because I couldn't be "real" with most of the women I was surrounded by. Even though this was conventional in a modern world, it was never considered acceptable by the Mormon church. And so, I felt like I had to hide

65

this part of myself so I could stay in good standing. So I could have their approval.

I remember one conversation with a Mormon friend where I was attempting to be open and honest about sex. Somehow, the topic shifted to what the church's guidelines were on "appropriate sex."

"I would *never* let my husband participate in oral sex," she had said with conviction. "That is inappropriate, and God would not approve of either of us doing that to one another. You should always invite God into your marriage and such acts disgust Him."

I remember stopping dead in my tracks at that comment. I had become paralyzed with fear. Was I sinning for exploring oral sex with my husband? Did God disapprove of me? Of our marriage?

Again, I felt like I had no control over my life. The Mormon church and the culture of its members had full control and manipulation over our physical relationship from the moment it began. Travis and I developed a fantastic emotional relationship from the start and still do to this day, but we were never allowed to explore our sexuality together prior to marriage because of the guilt attached to any physical affection beyond a simple kiss. And now, even in the sacred unity of marriage our love was being dictated.

I would be lying if I said this hasn't had lasting effects. My brain was manipulated into correlating sex and physical affection with sin—a sin that is so horrible, it is "next to murder." My brain was told over and over that my body was not my own and that it was a tool to create life. I was trained to turn my affection off. Almost completely. Because if I turned my affection on and we had premarital sex, I would be blamed for tempting a man into unrighteous behavior. I would be guilty of one of the worst sins in the eyes of God. I would be kicked out of school and put on spiritual probation. I would not be allowed to take the sacrament during services, I would have to attend meetings with my bishop as he fellowshipped me toward repentance. I would no longer be temple-worthy—my membership would be revoked. Our wedding would be delayed. Everyone would know.

I was taught that sex was something to be sorry for. So much shame. So much guilt. So much embarrassment. All for expressing love in a natural way.

Travis and I stayed celibate for ten months before we were married in the Columbia River Temple in Richland, Washington. And on our wedding day, a few fancy words were said and we were suddenly given permission to love one another sexually. We were encouraged to do so in the name of "multiplying and replenishing the earth."

I still feel my body become overwhelmed with anxiety when I think about this. I've been out of the church for many years but am still angry, grieving and frustrated. I hate that the church conditioned my young brain to feel anxiety and shame and guilt around sex. Around my own beautiful, strong body. I hate that in the beginning of our marriage it caused so much heartache for the both of us because I couldn't navigate sex in a healthy way.

I was terrified. I was confused about how my body was feeling and what my brain was simultaneously telling me. It was two very different things. My body was feeling warmth and love and safety but my brain was sending me into fight or flight. It made me hate myself. It made me spiral into self-loathing, which made me shut down completely. It made me unable to give or accept love.

A few weeks after our wedding, I wrote in my journal.

Dear Diary,

Last night I felt awful. Travis and I were starting to get intimate when my mind started racing, and I immediately started to cry and jumped up and left the room. I locked myself in the bathroom and cried. I felt horrible for doing that to Travis. He had no idea what was wrong.

Even I didn't know what was wrong. I couldn't verbalize it. I couldn't form thoughts around it. It was just… a feeling. The feeling that my body felt so much love and physical pleasure but that my brain felt extreme shame and embarrassment. Which left me alone in a bathroom crying, while my new husband sat outside the bathroom door with his head in his hands wondering what he did wrong and had no idea how to fix it.

Little did he know, there was nothing he *could* do. This was bigger than him. This was bigger than me. I didn't know I was struggling with trauma at the time, but now I do. And I feel so heartbroken for them—our past selves. They were just kids stuck in a fucking cult. And I was just Eunice, playing the part of a Mormon housewife and it felt all wrong. My body didn't feel like my own. I was uncomfortable in it, scared of it, ashamed of it. At the time I think my body and spirit were telling me everything the church had taught me was all wrong, but my brain was fighting it.

Today, I still have to actively turn my "affection switch" on. Whether I am giving hugs to a close friend or having an intimate moment with Travis, it is not something that comes naturally to me. I believe this is why writing has become such a passion for me. It is the one way I can truly express myself without feeling shame, embarrassment or awkwardness.

And it breaks my fucking heart.

People around me can interpret this as coldness, and sometimes Travis is even left feeling confused and frustrated about it needing to be such a conscious effort on my part. I try to explain but then I get frustrated because when I try to explain my conditioning to someone who wasn't as indoctrinated and controlled as I was it makes no sense. I don't expect it to. It doesn't make sense to me most days and that is why it is so hard to deconstruct. It takes real work and sometimes help from a professional to even make sense of it all. But I have found that as I have opened myself up to receive physical affection, it is easier for me to give it in return.

Sometimes, when I am processing the conditioning of my past, I let myself go back to that night in the potato field when Travis kissed me for the first time. We were in the back of his truck, snuggled in blankets. The crisp Idaho air reddened our cheeks. We were alone—not another soul for miles. That's the great thing about Idaho, you can actually drive to the middle of nowhere and seemingly disappear in a matter of minutes. I remember feeling simple contentment that night. Like every decision I had ever made led to that moment, laying under the stars with him. Our bodies had never been that close, and all I wanted was to show him how fast I was falling for him. The connection I felt with him was the most powerful force I'd ever experienced.

Finally, he sat up to look at me, and I just gazed at him with my whole heart wide open. The stars reflected their brilliant light in my eyes. When he slowly moved toward me, I knew I was about to be kissed by the love of my life. All the stars above us suddenly shined brighter, like the universe had been waiting for Travis and Lindsay to love one another.

After a few small but passionate kisses, Travis smiled at me and said, "We have to be careful, we can't go too far." I knew what he meant. I smiled in agreement. We both felt such a powerful connection at such a simple display of affection. We knew right then that we were in each other's lives for the long haul.

If I could go back to that night, I would risk it all. I would allow myself to go blind in love, stop thinking of eternal consequences, and be in that moment with him. I would go "too far." I would let our bodies and our passion and our connection guide us. I would step into my right as a woman to decide with her partner how we'd want our physical relationship to pan out.

But I can't go back, and I know that. There are days I am so angry for how the church has affected me. The religious abuse I endured has taken years to deconstruct and I still have quite a ways to go, especially when it comes to sex. I am still learning about my body. About how to feel safe inside of it. About how to show affection. About not turning off my affection switch. I am learning about the beauty and wonder that lies in the physical connection of a soulmate.

For years, I was a live wire caught in a puddle. I was self-destructive, charged, delicate, and my sense of direction was muddled. I was my own worst enemy and I kept looking toward my faith in the church to be my life raft. Little did I know, they were the ones in control of the power, and they weren't going to turn it off. In fact, they had supercharged me for this and now I am left alone to navigate the long-lasting effects of the purity culture they endorse.

I don't have a clear, definitive answer as to how to overcome these struggles. Everyone is different and everyone's needs are unique. However, having a patient partner is the best thing that has ever happened to me. As well as being patient with myself. Travis listens to me. He respects me. And he goes at my pace when needed. We communicate regularly, in an honest and loving way. And oh my God, it has been incredible!

We've worked through many frustrations and continue to do so as needed. It's beautiful. Every part of our life together has transformed into a true partnership. I love working together as a unified, cohesive force in a way that we both feel loved, valued and respected. As far as giving myself space to heal and having patience... that's been a challenge. But because I have a supportive partner, I am able to reflect, heal and move forward without feeling rushed or forced.

Healing from purity culture has been a painfully slow process but I do notice big changes in my behavior. I hug the people I love. I snuggle with my husband on the couch. I no longer have a knee jerk reaction to people touching me. I hold Travis' hand whenever I get the chance. I feel safe when we have sex. I feel open and connected to him instead of feeling like I am shrinking in on myself. I no longer panic at the hands of physical human connection.

It's been an incredibly painful process, and I wish I never had to go through it. I don't wish this on anyone. Human connection is healthy. As women, our bodies are *ours*. Our bodies do not belong to men. Our bodies are sexual, yes, but we are not in charge of anyone else's emotions, thoughts or actions surrounding our bodies. Period. Men are not held responsible for our sexual thoughts or actions, so why are we accountable for theirs?

This concept is toxic patriarchy at its finest. Another way to control women and force them into sexual submission. The sexual revolution of women is highly frowned upon by the church. We are showing them that we are no longer puppets in their play. We are cutting the puppet strings tying us to our patriarchal fate.

No longer will our bodies be used, abused and governed with absolute authority. No longer will we stand for our young girls being hyper sexualized to the point of their ultimate sexual suppression. No longer will we stand for the teachings that our bodies, our intimate connections, be used solely to create life. Our sexuality connects us to other humans. It is a healthy form of self-expression.

We are entering a new age of the human psyche. I think we are educating ourselves on the lasting effects of human connections and realizing how important it is to our overall health in every way. We are finally allowing ourselves to break the chains of shame, guilt and toxic conservatism around our sexuality. We are opening up and expanding our point of view.

It is a beautiful time to be a modern woman, but for me to fully embrace this there was still more that I needed to heal from. And in a way that would also require me to realign my beliefs.

Beliefs that had been ingrained. Deep.

illusions

*I couldn't heal while inside the institution
that conditioned me to believe
trusting someone else was truer
than trusting myself.*

Dear Diary,

*I am angry and sad. I don't want to write but I feel like I
should. Travis told me that in the past he's slept with other women.
I am a virgin and still have my innocence intact. I wish Travis
could stoop down to my level for a little while. He will never
understand the heartache it causes me. We will never have that
"first-time" connection. I get sick when I think of those other
women. Travis won't ever understand. I wish he could understand.
I wish he could have his memory erased of how it felt with them. I
wish I was the only one. I wish I was the only one that could ever
make him feel that way.*

What should I do now?

Nine days after writing this journal entry, Travis and I had
become engaged, which started the process of wedding planning
and temple worthiness interviews for both Travis and me. For
months, my only outlet for my grief had been my journal.

"I'm still so sad," I wrote. *"I don't know how to fix this
since I can't change his past. I'm praying for a softened heart
today."*

Over six months of our engagement, I had had extreme
highs and very low lows. Eventually, I took to calling my lowest

73

moments of anxiety, "the bad thing," which was essentially my name for a panic attack that would ensue over Travis' previous relationships. I had become obsessed with trying to understand how someone could show this kind of sacred love outside of a marriage union. I just couldn't wrap my brain around it, because it had been drilled into me for *years* that this sin was "second to murder."

Second to *murder*!

Ultimately, I had become convinced that his past intimacy meant he could never fully love me. But then I wondered if I was projecting my own feelings onto him. Maybe, I couldn't love Travis fully until I deconditioned the toxic belief systems that had been engrained into me. Maybe I had been taught to fear sex so much that my nervous system was having a survival response.

In June 2011, I wrote, *Suddenly, it was as if I was in a nightmare. It was as if I knew and loved Travis dearly only to find out that he has never been, and never will be, mine. When I am with Travis I feel safe. When he's gone I feel so insecure... so alone. I feel helpless at times... like I am fighting a battle that I can't win because I can't change his past. Why does it bother me? Why do I let it bother me? I don't want the Travis that was with them. I want the Travis that is with me. I have him, yet I still let it bother me. I hate talking to him about it. Most of the time, I cry and make a fool out of myself. It makes him upset also. I don't try to make him feel bad or worthless, but sometimes I just feel worthless. What could I offer him that he hasn't already had? I don't know if I'll ever know the answer to that question.*

The illusion here is that I had believed everything I was taught, and Travis was challenging that core belief. The belief that when you are intimate you are giving something away that can

74

never be returned. The belief that love can only happen with one person. The belief that your worth is tied to sex.

I have pages and pages of my journals filled with this grief. They are filled with tears of a young woman trying to make sense of it all. Trying to make sense of love that challenged the belief systems that had been drilled into her for years. Ultimately, I decided back then that I needed help, so I turned to the person I had been taught to turn to in times like these—my bishop. The most trusted man in the Mormon flock.

Travis and I had an appointment with our bishop for a temple worthiness interview as we had made further preparations for our temple wedding. Travis went first and a few minutes later he exited the room. The bishop had given him a firm handshake and a pat on the back—the kind of pat a proud father gives to his son.

I went next.

The interview went well, and as we wrapped up I stumbled through the words I had needed to say. The words that I had filled my journal pages with. The words that had caused me so much pain and confusion. The entire time, I stared at my lap and felt my face warm with nervousness. When I was done there was a brief pause and then the bishop spoke.

"Your Savior doesn't recognize his sin, so neither should you," he had said bluntly.

I sat directly across from him, eyes downcast, trembling inside. My sweaty fingers intertwined with one another fiddling faster and faster as the internal panic rose inside my chest.

"Bishop, I understand that," I had squeaked almost silently. "But I am just having a really difficult time emotionally. I know he's repented but he's slept with other women, and I've never been with anyone in that way. I guess I just need guidance."

"Listen, Lindsay, this will not get better by talking about it. Once you leave this office you should never speak of it again—to anyone. Especially Travis. You are lucky to have a man like him." He stood from behind his desk and opened the door. That had been my cue to leave.

I am lucky to have a man like him. I am lucky to have a man like him. I am lucky to have a man like him. I repeated this over and over to myself as I walked home, and for days after. One night, alone in my apartment, I wrote this entry in my journal:

My Bishop told me to never bring up Travis' past sins to Travis or anyone. I have followed his advice completely. It's so hard. I've never had anything in my life affect me this much. I want to go to therapy to deal with it, but I also want to keep following my Bishop's advice to never talk about it to anyone. I don't want this to affect us. I have no clue why it tears me apart like it does, but it makes me physically sick. I feel like I am going in circles with myself. I have to fight it every day. I feel like a small but significant part of me has shut off. I have been trying to use my faith and let the atonement work on me. I love Travis more than anything and I am willing to do whatever it takes to get through this. I just don't feel like myself.

Reading this almost 10 years later brings an all-familiar ache to my heart. I was a 19-year-old woman drowning in deep fear. Honestly, I don't know if "woman" is even accurate. I was still very much a child in many ways. After all, for years I had been taught to correlate sex with chewed gum. No one wants a piece of chewed gum, right? And after years of being told that I would be nothing but a piece of chewed gum if I had premarital sex, now my bishop was telling me that Travis was whole and fresh and unchewed. That I was lucky to have a man like him. All he had to do was say sorry and it was like it never happened.

But it did happen, and I was not mentally or emotionally prepared to navigate this kind of "game," one that trained me to both fear and accept sex at the same time based on the rules that the church had laid out for young women. This "game" that taught me to hold my virginity to the highest standard, while forgiving the man who gave his away.

Up until this point in my life, I viewed sexuality as merely a tool to create life—nothing more. My young brain had been conditioned to see sex and intimacy as a sin outside of marriage. And my fiancé had committed that sin with other women.

How could I *possibly* move forward without guidance? The truth is that I didn't. I couldn't. Because before I could do that, I'd have to undo 10 years' worth of conditioning. I'd have to realize the illusion that sat before me. I'd have to rebel against everything that I had been taught.

I'd have to get help.

I loved Travis more than anything. That I knew without a doubt. I fell in love with him so fast. He became my best friend, my confidant, a breath of fresh air to my soul in a matter of months. He became my person. And yet, he had committed a sin that was next to murder—or so I thought.

And when I sought help to navigate this from a trusted leader, I was brushed aside and told how lucky I was to have a man like him. My feelings about the matter were not seen or accepted as being valid. My feelings about the matter were not considered to be important. My feelings about the matter were to never be spoken of again.

Almost a decade later I can now say that marrying that "sinner" was the best decision I've ever made. One thing the bishop said that day was true—I *am* lucky to have a man like him, but he's also lucky to have *me*.

The illusion that manifested before me was that Travis had committed a serious sin. One that had been drilled into my brain from the age of 13. One that was so serious it was almost unforgivable in the eyes of God. But I, his fiancée, his eternal companion, was expected to simply *get over it*. No questions asked. No fuss made. A non-issue. Do I even dare to wonder what this would have been like if the roles had been reversed?

What if I had slept with multiple men and my fiancé was a virgin? What if he was struggling and brought this issue to the bishop for advice on how to move forward? Would this bishop, or the church for that matter, still see this as a non-issue? Would I, a female, receive the proud dad backslap and a firm handshake? Or would my fiancé be called in to council me? And would I have to take further steps to correct this… issue?

Lastly, would Travis be told that he was "lucky to have a *woman* like me?"

What I've learned since then is that when it comes to deciphering our own hearts, separating truth from illusion is arguably the most difficult mystery to solve. And recently, I've begun to wonder if maybe we all have *truthful* illusions. Truths that are the most valid and tangible realities during a part of our lives, but in hindsight are easily recognizable as a mere illusion. A laughable fantasy we lived. A toxic expectation we required of ourselves. A traumatic period of our lives that held a lot of weight to decisions we made. Maybe even another life we lived that seems so distant now.

These truthful illusions are powerful, mighty things. They contort our reality to fit the mold of the life we're currently living. Truthful illusions are designed by things like religion, family values, historical constructs, economic status and a myriad of other impactful things. Ultimately, they are the scope we see from for a limited time before learning the real truth.

What I was faced with after leaving the bishop's office that day was that I had to choose healing—but I couldn't heal by staying silent. Which meant that I couldn't heal inside the institution that conditioned me to believe trusting someone else was truer than trusting myself.

What my heart was telling me was much different than the illusion my brain had been conditioned to believe. My heart was telling me that Travis had not committed a sin next to murder. My heart was telling me that Travis was innocent in all of this. And yet my brain had become so obsessed with the sin that I couldn't love Travis fully.

Glennon Doyle puts my emotions into words perfectly by saying, *Wait. This thing I have been taught to believe about God, about myself, about others—it doesn't fit with what I know from my roots about love. What do I do? Do I reject what I know from my roots or what I was taught to believe?*

My indoctrination was leaving me incapable of loving someone else to the extent that my heart wanted to love him. And I'll be damned if I love a church, organization, or other entity more than I love another human being.

A few years later, following a conversation with Travis, I had such a powerful revelation it knocked me off my feet and onto my knees. God is *not* the church. God is *not* that bishop. God is *not* the temple. God is *within* me. God has *always* been within me, and always *will* be.

That's when I took my power back. My power to choose love and life over a man-made organization. My power to form independent thought free from every rule and expectation and guideline I had ever been taught to follow. The illusion washed away with my ownership of power, and I felt physical weight shift off my shoulders. Tears stained my cheeks for weeks. Months.

But before I could learn any of this, before I could love him and myself fully, I had to become Eunice. I had to take the bishop's advice and apply it to my life. I had to become silent, submissive and fully go through the motions of becoming a good Mormon wife. I had to embody the meek, kind and nurturing role of the woman I had been trained to be from the moment I came out of the baptismal font.

the last covenant

I was coming face to face with the reality
that my eternity would be separate from theirs
just like my wedding ceremony was.
They'd be in heaven's waiting room, while I was inside.

"Who here has had to defy someone or something to do what you know to be right?" my BYU-I college professor had asked. Almost every hand in the stuffy lecture hall raises instantly, and with angst. Including mine.

I looked around the room. Every single person sitting beside me looked the same, spoke the same, and believed in the same values. The same doctrine. The same culture. All the girls were dressed beyond Mormon modesty standards—a standard everyone at the university understood.

The private Mormon institution has its own set of standards, which were even more rigid than typical. No sandals, no shorts, no unnatural hair color, no tight jeans, no sweatpants, no leggings, no beards, no hats. A gym uniform was given to each student and admittance into the weight room was allowed only if this uniform was worn. Anyone who rolled their sleeves up was immediately told to roll them back down or they'd be forced to leave. Girls seen wearing dresses or skirts above the knee would be told to leave class. Men dawning beards were sent home to shave. Repeat offenders were reported to the student honor code office where their futures at the school were decided.

Once, during a math final I had been interrupted by a testing center attendant and told to pull my shirt down over my lower back. Embarrassed, I had quickly sat up to adjust my shirt. I was told if I broke the rules again, I would be sent home with half my final complete and that my teacher would be notified. My face had lit up red with shame. I had been so focused on my final that I didn't even realize my shirt had come up. Math had always been a familiar enemy of mine, numbers have never made sense to me. My anxiety around this test had been building for weeks, and after that embarrassing moment I had never regained focus. Instead, it had taken all of my energy to hold back hot tears. Afterwards, I had ran back to my apartment crying from shame, embarrassment and anger. This was my educational institution. This was my life. In order to stay away from the shame, I had to be the same as everyone else. I had to conform to the standards of the university.

"Now," my professor continued with conviction, "which one of you would be willing to share a story from a time when you had to choose the right, even if it was an unpopular decision?"

Everyone looked around at each other, wondering who would be the first to go. I slowly raised my hand again and the professor called on me immediately.

"I was just sealed to my husband in the temple a few weeks ago," I said. "None of our families could attend because they aren't members."

Everyone's eyes were suddenly on me. People were turning around in their seats to stare at the recently sealed Mormon convert that had defied worldly values and instead did as the church told her to do.

"That's quite impressive!" the professor said. "This is a fantastic example!" He was giddy now, my example fit perfectly into his lesson plan. "What you did takes a lot of courage. Who here would have the courage to do what she did?"

Silently, I stared around the room as the majority of hands raised immediately. The rest looked down at their laps.

"Those of you who didn't raise your hand, can you explain why?" the professor asked. Slowly, a girl in the front of the room raised her hand.

"I'm sorry, but I just couldn't do that," she looked back at me sympathetically as she spoke. "My mom means everything to me, and I could never get married without her there." I nodded my head in understanding. I, too, had a mom that meant everything to me. And I, too, couldn't believe I had gotten married without her there.

"I understand," I said smiling gently at her.

For the rest of class my mind left my body sitting there still as a statue, taking me back to my wedding day—just two weeks prior.

It had been 4am and my alarm was blaring. A half dozen sleeping girls laid around the room in the same configuration as a crossword puzzle. The night before we had stayed up late excitedly chatting away about that day—the day I married Travis.

I had slept in old basketball shorts and a Batman t-shirt that I had bought a few years back at Walmart for the midnight movie premier. I had stood in line for almost four hours prior to the movie starting with some of the girls that were now splayed across my bedroom floor. That night we had snuck junk food into the theater and even tried an energy drink for the first time. These girls had grown up with goofy little Lindsay, and now they were going to watch her become Mrs. Helm. A *woman*.

I had changed clothes and remembered I was wearing garments. A symbol of status in Mormon culture. The day before I had gone through my endowment ceremony, where I received my new name and new underwear. It was one of the first nights I had slept in them. A small smile formed as I felt a wave of pride flow over me. Here I was checking off every box of a righteous young woman. I was wearing garments just like I was supposed to, and now I was going to become someone's wife!

I had woken the other girls and we piled into the car with my mom to head over for hair and makeup at my grandma's house. I had wanted to get ready in my childhood home, surrounded by the people I loved most.

A few hours later, I heard a deep voice echoing down the hallway. Travis was there! Perfect timing. My hair and makeup had just been finished and my wedding dress was on. My mom had directed him to the backyard and a few minutes later I made my way down to him. With his back turned to me, I had gently tapped his shoulder and watched his face light up with joy. He was so handsome in his fitted grey suit. His caramel skin glowed in the summer sunshine. I couldn't believe we were about to get married!

We had arrived at the temple with our ceremonial clothes in hand—the clothes we would change into for the sealing. We had to have one last interview before we could move forward. This time it was with the temple president.

"Good morning, Travis and Lindsay," he had said as he welcomed us into his ornate temple office.

"Good morning!" we said in unison, giggling nervously.

We had sat in plush white chairs facing the temple president, who sat behind a large mahogany desk. A framed picture of Jesus had been mounted on the wall behind him, keeping a watchful eye.

"How are you both feeling?"

I spoke first and it came out like a tidal wave that filled every surface, corner and cranny of the room.

"Excited!" I shouted, much too loud for inside the Lord's house.

The temple president chuckled softly, like a serene woodland creek flowing purposefully through the forest floor.

"I can see that," he smiled.

After the temple president had interviewed us and deemed us worthy to be sealed, Travis and I went our separate ways to change into our ceremonial clothes.

Even though my wedding gown had been modest, I had not been allowed to wear it into the temple. Mormon temples have strict modesty guidelines that prohibit almost any skin from showing, and embellishments of any kind are frowned upon. Temple clothes are also not allowed to be worn outside of the temple, so I had worn church clothes to enter the temple and changed into my temple dress for the sealing.

In the locker room I had slipped into my floor length temple dress, pulled on white knee-high stockings, and slipped into my white silk slippers. I had fashioned my temple veil to my hair, which covered my face and neck during the ceremony. My robe looked exactly like a Greek toga that you'd wear to a sorority party, and my apron was dark green and embroidered to look like leaves from the garden of Eden.

With my ceremonial clothes on, the locker room attendant had led me to the celestial room, where Travis had been waiting for me. He too, was dressed in his ceremonial clothes. The thick carpet made no sound beneath our slippers as we walked to one of the most sacred rooms for temple-worthy Latter-Day Saints. I had felt both a sense of peace and sadness overcome me. I could not wait to marry my soulmate but had longed for my and Travis' families to be by our sides.

As Travis saw me walk in, he stood up from the round sofa he was sitting on in the middle of the enormous. We smiled at each other and I joined him. Together we waited, holding hands and taking in the beauty of the surrounding room. It was one of the most beautiful rooms I'd ever seen.

White carpet adorned with gold leafed trim, marble pillars stood 20 feet high, and stained-glass windows depicted the three kingdoms of heaven. A tall white veil had cloaked one side of the giant room, and on the other side of the veil was where the endowment ceremony takes place. This is where temple-goers make covenants with God for both themselves and the dead. During this ceremony each person walks toward the veil and as instructed puts their right hand inside a small slit where it was held by a man on the other side. There, the man reads from a script and both parties show the required signs and tokens, which are handshakes, to be ushered through the veil and symbolically into heaven.

That day, I had been so happy to be in the celestial room without having to do the endowment ceremony. I'd only done it once, but it was long and confusing. I wasn't really sure what to make of it. I honestly had felt like a fish out of water during my endowment. The only part that made any sense was sitting in the beauty of the celestial room afterwards and feeling a sense of peace talking to God. And that morning I had been overjoyed to be sitting in the celestial room with my soon-to-be husband, taking in the peace and serenity of the Lord's house.

After several minutes of waiting, I started to get antsy. We shouldn't have been waiting this long, I had thought. I felt that something was wrong. We hadn't seen another temple worker in quite some time. There wasn't a single clock in the celestial room, but I had known it was past the time we had been scheduled for our sealing.

Finally, I got up and left the celestial room to look for someone. Immediately, I saw an elderly woman walking towards me. She put her hands up gently to stop me from going any further.

"There's been a little problem," she had said nervously. I could tell she was trying to maintain the joy that should have been surrounding that day, but there was a tone of concern in her voice. And instead of calming me, it scared me.

"What's going on?" I asked.

"Well, it seems your father is a bit distressed, so the temple president is down there now speaking to him."

My heart sunk.

My entire family was in that waiting room. Travis' entire family was in that waiting room. Because they weren't temple-worthy active members of the LDS church, they weren't permitted to go any further than the waiting room. None of them could have watched us be married in the temple, that is why I bought a wedding dress and we had planned for a ring ceremony afterwards in my grandparents' backyard—even though it had not been encouraged.

Wasn't that enough?

I went back into the celestial room and sat down next to Travis. He felt my heaviness instantly. The grandness of the room suddenly had felt too big. I wished I didn't feel so alone in making a choice I felt was right for us. This was the only way Travis and I could be together forever—by being sealed in the temple. That meant more to me than anything, but it didn't negate the fact that I still had wished our families were there to love and support us on our big day. I felt conflicted. Angry. Confused. Sad.

"He's trying to ruin my day," I whispered to Travis.

87

"What are you talking about?" he asked.

"My dad is throwing a fit in the waiting room and the temple president is down there talking to him. That's why we've been waiting this long."

"Oh..." he said looking down at his lap, knowing his own family was also down there. Tears had swelled in my eyes as he reached his arm around me and pulled me close.

"Everything will be okay."

My stomach had churned as I fought back hot tears. After some time, the overwhelming waves of conflicting emotions I felt caused me to completely shut down. On my wedding day, I just could not face them. So instead, I closed my eyes and flipped a switch inside my brain—much like turning a light switch off. The anger I felt toward my dad—off. The sadness I felt because I wanted him and every single person in that waiting room to join us—off. The embarrassment for having a member of my family make such a scene in a sacred space—off. The frustration because no one, especially not my dad, had known exactly why we chose to be married in the temple, and subsequently left them out—off.

One feeling, however, had remained on—internal conflict.

Conflicted because, if we didn't have a temple sealing, we'd be frowned upon by the church and we wouldn't be together forever, but our families would have been happier than they were in that waiting room. Conflicted because, my relationship with my dad was not the strongest, yet I've always wanted it to better and this had thrown a huge wrench in things. Conflicted because he and everyone else down there had six months to express themselves about our decision to be sealed in the temple and it all came to a boil on what was supposed to be the happiest day of our lives.

And all at once, at only 19 years old, and on my wedding day, I felt like I had let every single person I loved down. Every person that I loved most had been demoted to a waiting room instead of being by our side. I was in a lose-lose situation. If I walked out of that temple unsealed, I would be a disappointment in the church's eyes. If I walked out of the temple sealed, I would disappoint all the people I loved by leaving them out of our wedding ceremony.

I leaned into Travis' body more, knowing that physical affection was not encouraged in the temple. But I didn't care because I needed to syphon strength to regain my composure and focus on us—Travis and me. That was what I was there for. That was the start of the rest of our lives—our eternity.

A few minutes later a temple worker told us it was time to go to the sealing room. Travis and I squeezed hands and shared an excited smile before we left the celestial room and walked hand in hand to a small room right next door. When we walked into the sealing room, our witnesses had been waiting for us. My Mormon grandma was the first person I saw, before my two cousins who were also converts, and across the room stood our college friends who had been recently sealed together. My heart was so happy to be surrounded by these people, but the room had felt empty without the rest of our families there.

The temple sealer directed us toward the alter in the middle of the room. It was padded and about knee high, so Travis and I both knelt down and held hands across it. I was asked to cover my face with the veil—I did as I was told. Even after the sealer had begun to speak, the switch inside my brain remained off. All I saw was Travis. All I heard was the beating of my own heart. All I felt was the shaking of our joined hands. The sealer spoke, but I could not hear him until he said, "from this day forward do you agree to harken unto your husband as he hearkens unto the Lord?"

"Yes," I said.

Then we were directed to stand and look into the mirrors which are intentionally hung facing one another to create an eternal looking glass. We watched our image continue one after the other in the eternal spectrum and smiled. It was symbolic of our eternal love and our future eternal family that would be sealed together forever.

We knelt back down on the alter and were permitted one small kiss. We happily obliged and stood together, for the first time, as a married couple.

We hugged all six of the people in the room and went back to the locker rooms to change out of our ceremonial clothes. At this point, I was permitted to change into my real wedding dress, but first, the temple worker told me to go see my parents in the waiting room. I agreed, although I had been nervous to see my dad. All I wanted was for him to respect my wishes and be happy for me. But I also knew that he was hurting, and it couldn't have been easy for him to sit in that room while I got married.

I put my robe, veil and apron back in my locker, which left me in my white temple dress. My discomfort had grown with every step I took toward the waiting room. I walked down the staircase and through the magnificent foyer to the waiting room. My dress had made me look like an angel gliding through heaven's gates.

There, alone, sat my mom and dad. Everyone else had left.

They both looked up at as I entered. My mom's eyes lit up and she smiled. My dad hardly recognized me in my dress with my hair and makeup done.

"Wow punk, you look beautiful!" he said, calling me by the nickname he'd used for me since I was a child.

"Hi, honey. How did it go?" my mom had asked.

I looked at my parents, who created me and who I loved. I saw them sitting there alone in that room while their only daughter got married upstairs in a room they were not allowed into. I saw myself making a choice I had been taught to believe was good and holy and sacred, but it was also a choice that didn't include the people that I loved. It was a choice that caused not only joy, but pain. Pain not just for them, but for me too.

As I had stood in the waiting room with them, I felt nothing. I felt nothing because every wire in my brain was contradicting itself, so I turned it off. My belief system had been challenged and uprooted, and I had come face to face with the reality that my eternity would be separate from theirs, just like my wedding ceremony had been.

They'd be in heaven's waiting room, while I would be inside.

Suddenly, my dad spoke. He shifted uncomfortably as he tried to remain calm, but I had sensed his tone.

"So… you like all this, huh, punk?" he asked.

I looked down at my white slippers and shifted my feet.

"Yeah, I guess… I do," I said. "I do."

trauma

It is heaven and it is hell. It is good and it is evil.
It is submission and it is rebellion.
It is a host of horrors and God's essence.
It is me.

Long before I'd met Travis, I had a nightmare while studying at BYU-I. At this point in my life, thanks to the student honor code and living in a place where everyone's beliefs were the same as my own, I was the most indoctrinated as I'd ever been. I was on the fast track to Eunice. The church was no longer just about church on Sunday—it was engrained into every waking minute of my day. And this time, it had even made itself into my dreams.

In this particular dream, I was both in my body and outside of it. I was both living as me and watching myself like an actor in her very own movie. It was my wedding day and I was surrounded by marble floors and gold leafed everything. Pillars of solid, gleaming stone cascaded from the high ceilings down to the floor. Stained glass windows separated where I stood in the celestial realm from the outside world.

Everything was illuminated, white, brilliant—like heaven. I'd never seen anything so beautiful in my entire life. I felt like I was royalty, standing in her castle, and was overwhelmed with sacred duty. I stood alone, steadfast with purpose, taking it all in. I felt like I'd made it. I'd finally proven my worth. I was good enough to be there, in the Lord's house, to be sealed for time and all eternity. I felt like I'd passed a test—the omnipotent kind.

I took a deep breath and relaxed my shoulders.

93

Finally.

I did it.

The delicate ends of my mouth turned upwards into a small smile. But just as I breathed easy, something dark caught my eye and I glanced down. My smile flattened as I grew concerned. What could possibly contrast so much illuminating beauty? My eyes followed the darkness, and I saw that the darkness was on the hem of my long, white temple dress.

Reactively, I attempted to step away from it. I was repulsed by it. I did not want any part of it. It had no place here— not in this sacred space.

Not within me.

But when I stepped away, the black chiffon glided over the marble floors like a demonic shadow. The darkness was attached to my dress. When I moved, it moved. Suddenly, I had felt like I was in a horror movie. Panicked, I looked up in search of help. Surely someone must be here—a temple worker, a friend, God? But as my eyes searched the heavenly castle where I stood, I saw a colossal, golden mirror that had been placed in my path, and I was faced with my own reflection.

A reflection that took my breath away.

A reflection that left me horrified.

There, alone in the Lord's house, in my sacred castle, I saw myself clothed in darkness and in light. Half of my dress was a heavenly white and the other half was dark as the midnight sky. Split directly down the middle, my dress was a contradiction. It was heaven and it was hell. It was good and it was evil. It was submission and it was rebellion. It was a host of horrors and God's essence.

It was me.

When I woke, I was covered in tears. I knelt by my bed and prayed. But I knew. I already knew.

At the time, I was convinced it was a message from God—and not the good kind. I was certain he was warning me. He was tapping on the shoulder of my soul issuing a stern reminder that I had work to do. That He could see me. He could hear my thoughts and whisperings of my heart.

He knew.

He knew I was not as devout as I said I was. He knew I had doubts about the truthfulness of the church. He knew I ever so secretly wished I'd never been baptized but didn't have the strength nor critical thinking abilities to get out on my own. And He knew that I continually swallowed those thoughts in an effort to be more faithful. To be good. To endure to the end.

But now, as I look back on this, I have an additional interpretation of the dream. Maybe this dream came from God, or maybe it was from my own soul that I had betrayed and locked away in the dungeon of my subconsciousness.

Either way, the message is clear to me now.

There is nothing more truthful than my own reflection. Even as I stood in the Lord's house, the most holy place on earth, I was faced with myself. All of myself. The darkness and the light. My doubts and my faith. My longing to be free and my willingness to submit in an effort of eternal salvation. And my reflection terrified me. My reflection forced me to see myself as I really am. My reflection cannot be hidden, suppressed or unacknowledged. My reflection is true. And as I searched for someone, anyone to help me escape the darkness that seemed to follow me, who did I find there in that celestial space?

I did not find God. I did not find a friend. I did not find the man I was there to marry. I found me. I was there to confront myself. To no longer betray myself. To remind myself that no matter what I did, or where I went, the only one who could truly help me, love me, save me, was myself. I was there living out a fear. The fear that no matter what I did, I was not "enough." And that fear was reflected back to me. There was no running from it. There was no hiding from it. Because it was a part of me. A part of my true reflection. A part of my soul.

My indoctrination at the time fed into this fear of enoughness. It kept me from seeing the dream clearly. Instead, I saw the dream as a punishment. As a vision into the future if I didn't shape up. The indoctrination had told me that it was my fault. That even on the happiest day of my life, I would not be good enough to marry the man of my dreams in the house of the Lord.

And God would know.

I carried this dream around with me for years. It was like a tiny devil on my shoulder. Whenever I'd remember it, I'd go down the rabbit hole of anxiety. I was ashamed that God had to send me a stern message like that. I had blamed myself and vowed to try harder to be better.

For years before leaving the church this kind of internal conflict became my norm. I became a master at hiding any doubts. I enthusiastically accepted callings like adult Sunday school teacher, vice president of Relief Society, family history teacher and ward missionary. I felt like if I was called to serve in these ways, the Lord must be pleased with me. But it was also a chance for me to prove myself. I wanted Him and everyone around me to believe that I was all in. That I was inherently good and deserving of blessings. I wanted myself to believe it too.

Ward members began to notice my dedication and would commend me on being such a good example to them.

"Your faith is such an example to me," they would say.

I would smile and say thank you and try to end the conversation because I would see "her" again if I let it go on. I would see me in the dress of darkness and light, a faithful fraud. It would happen like a flash. One second she's there and the next she's gone—there to remind me who I *really* was, and who I was running away from.

I realize now that the root of these fears, and showing up with large red flags in ablaze, was Religious Trauma Syndrome (RTS). RTS is defined as a group of symptoms that arise in response to traumatic or stressful religious experiences. It is a common experience shared among many who have escaped cults, fundamentalist religious groups, abusive religious settings or other painful experiences with religion. Professionals says the symptoms of RTS are comparable to the symptoms of complex PTSD.

The symptoms I experienced over the years have been:

- confusing thoughts and reduced ability to think critically
- negative beliefs about self, others, and the world
- trouble making decisions
- feelings of depression, anxiety, grief, anger, lethargy
- sense of feeling lost, directionless, and alone
- lack of pleasure or interest in things you used to enjoy
- loss of a community (family, friends, romantic relationships)
- feeling isolated or a sense that you don't belong
- feeling "behind the times" with cultural happenings
- nightmares, flashbacks, dissociation, emotional difficulty

Through talk therapy, self-help books, podcasts, journaling and the support of family, close friends, and connecting with other post-Mormons through online communities, I have been able to navigate my way through RTS to find healing. Many of us have found similarities and common ground in our faith transitions through speaking about the effect it's had on our mental health. The rest of the world, however, is still somewhat in the dark.

"What if I told you that what you're experiencing isn't religious trauma, but a consequence of sin and disobedience?" I was once asked. "When we stop praying for protection against the Adversary, he will begin to sift us like wheat from the chaff. Have faith. Read the *Book of Mormon*. Pray."

As of late, it seems there has been a pandemic happening in the post-Mormon and ex-evangelical community. They are so terrified of the toxic church culture of shame, blame and ostracism that they would rather take their own lives than leave the church and risk losing it all.

As a member of the post-Mormon community who has watched dozens upon dozens of grieving parents, friends and allies share their stories of loss, I feel a responsibility to shine a light on it. As heartbreaking and uncomfortable as it is, it *has* to be talked about. We are losing incredible humans who have love and light and goodness to share in this world. But they are dying. Due to extreme orthodox practices, cultures of sameness and overbearing religious structures, the scriptures out of which they preach become the actual weapon in these dying people's hands.

Some of these individuals see no way out, no way to live their own truth outside of the religious organization they have been raised in, and so to them there is no other choice. Either they continue to live a lie in a system intoxicating their mind and bodies or they take themselves out of the equation all together.

They'd rather die than be gay. They'd rather die than admit they aren't happy in their marriages or in their religion. They'd rather die than be disowned by their families. They'd rather die than risk losing their community, part of their identity, the love they so deserve.

They'd rather die.

But is a human life worth more than religion? Is a human life worth more than meeting an organization's standards of righteousness? Is a human life worth more than the gospel? Is a human life worth more than a religion's version of God?

How much is a human life worth? Is a Mormon soul worth more than all the others? Is a post-Mormon soul worth less? Why isn't anyone talking about this? Why aren't religions who claim to be spreading the love of God and Jesus actually *saving* people? Why do they continue to turn a blind eye, point fingers, and call names? Why do I hear prophets of God calling us "lazy learners" and "lax disciples," when all we want is to be seen, heard, held and loved?

I wonder what would happen if our world was not so black and white, us against them. I wonder what would happen if we stopped trying to fit into prefabricated molds that are much too small for our growing spirits.

As I think about the people suffering, losing their lives, battling demons—I think about the girl who was becoming Eunice. The girl clothed in a dress of darkness and light. There was a time where she could've lost it all, but the people in her life wouldn't let her go. Whether she stayed on the path of Mormon exaltation or chose the path of her soul—she would've always been surrounded by unconditional love.

Another message has become clear to me since the night I had that dream. As I stood there in the Lord's temple, where everything was white, except for some gold leafing, the darkness took over me and I was in a world where everything, including me, was black and white. There was no gray. There was no rainbow of brilliant colors. Just illuminating white and deep, black darkness. And when living in a world of black and white doesn't just haunt your dreams, but is your reality, there's no room for growth.

Growth lies in the rainbow of brilliant colors and in the ability to see goodness in all its forms.

This dream taught me that my past muted world of black and white is now a rainbow of magical purples and blues and reds and yellows. And while I originally thought that dream was a punishment, now I think it might have been a loving warning. A warning that I was living in the black and white. That I was going down a road with no room for my soul's growth. No room for my rainbow spirit to burst free, live wildly, profoundly and creatively. Maybe the dream was supposed to scare me for a reason, because in my soul I knew I could never live in a muted world. In a world where my soul would be caged and I could not shine.

garden beds

My husband has left our garden box.
The box that keeps us safe.
The box that keeps us together forever.

I'm a below average gardener and yet I find absolute joy in it. Which is funny, being the perfectionist that I am. Being mediocre in this hobby of mine doesn't bother me one bit, though. It's quite literally a growing experience for everyone and everything involved.

During my second season of black-thumbed cultivation, my husband built a beautifully raised bed and hauled four yards of organic mixed-compost garden soil from our driveway all the way to the back yard where the garden bed lives. This is how he shows his love. Even though he knew deep in his big squishy heart that minimal veggies would come out alive, he still supported my vision.

Each year since, I've planted an abundance of veggies and herbs. I feel so much peace when I'm out there with my little plant babies, nurturing them, talking to them and watching them grow. It's been a phenomenal learning experience, and by that I mean I mess up way more than I succeed.

When I first started I threw some seeds into the soil, gave it a squirt of H2O, said a prayer to the rain and veggie gods, and walked away. But as it turns out, there's more to it. Who woulda thought? It also turns out that some veggie plants need more space than others. Duh, right? And you would never guess but it *also* turns out that some plants can't be planted near the other plants— not in the same soil, not in the same garden bed, not even in the same airspace. I didn't learn this until my third year of trying to grow a garden in my beautifully raised bed. Up until that point, a plant was a plant. Besides, they all require the same things—soil, sun and water.

What could be so hard about gardening?

One day I decided to grow delicious Walla Walla onions. These bad boys are staples in my kitchen. Growing up in eastern Washington, Walla Walla sweet onions were on the A-list of veggies. The Jennifer Garner of every dinner plate. They're sweet and make everyone happy—I've never met a single person who didn't like them.

I decided to research these tasty morsels of sweet onion heaven since I'd never attempted to grow any kind of onion before. Turns out they should never, under any circumstances, be planted next to beans. Which I was also growing. Okay, I thought, no big deal. I'd just plant them somewhere else in the garden bed.

So, I arranged and planted my garden soon after. It turned out beautiful. All the little plant babies were thriving. It was like watching a dozen baby Groot's dance in the sunshine, growing their happy roots and drinking the fertilizer Kool-Aid.

Cucumbers, zucchinis, onions, brussels sprouts, tomatoes, green beans and eggplant were all in their place.

I felt so accomplished!

Feeling like that was the best garden yet, I decided to do a little more research on my plants to ensure I was providing the best life possible for them. I went onto Google and started typing away. I started with the brussels sprouts.

"How To Grow Brussels Sprouts," I typed.

100,000 search results?

I clicked on the first article I saw. Turns out brussels sprouts are easy to grow. Great! They especially love zone 8B. My zone! Thank you, sweet baby brussels sprout Jesus.

I read on.

Scroll.

Scroll.

Scroll.

Then something caught my eye.

"Under no circumstances should brussels sprouts be planted anywhere near peppers." My face turned white. Oh no!

I swear to the Gardening God Almighty that the Master Gardeners of the internet were screaming at me through the computer. I had made a huge mistake.

Guess where my brussels sprouts had been planted? Right next to my goddamn peppers.

I kept reading in horror.

"If planted next to peppers, brussels sprouts will inhibit the peppers growth. In fact, they should not be planted in the same garden bed *at all*."

I took a deep breath and tried not to panic. Dear God, what have I done? Planting my brussels sprouts next to my peppers meant only one thing—certain pepper death. After a few seconds of letting this sink in I started to panic but kept reading.

"Brussels sprouts are in the cabbage family, which is toxic to nightshades like peppers and tomatoes. Peppers and brussels sprouts will compete for nutrients in the soil. They are otherwise known as 'garden enemies.'"

Garden *enemies*?

So, what the great and knowledgeable gardeners of the vast and ever-knowing internet were trying to teach me is that just because a veggie is a veggie doesn't mean it is the same veggie as the veggie next to it.

In other words, just because they are planted in the same garden, require most of the same things to survive, and on a cellular level have the same way of creating and manifesting their own fruits—they are not compatible. They are enemies of the highest veggie degree.

I slouched in my chair feeling very *very* sorry for myself. It was too late to replant, and I honestly didn't have the room to accommodate for this new veggie drama.

That night, I went to bed like I usually did—swimming in deep thought and anxiety and all the great things that make us human but are not good for sleeping. But it got me to thinking, what if we are all planted in the same proverbial soil and given the same nutrients and just expected to grow just as tall and strong as the plant next to us with any regard to how other plants may be toxic to *our* growth. What then?

And what if we cultivate new plants of our own making and give them everything we've been given—the same soil, the same water, the same sunlight—and expect them to grow just as big and tall and happy, never wondering if maybe they need something different. Never wondering if they may even need to grow in their own garden bed.

That will never happen, right?

When I chose to plant myself in the garden bed of Mormonism, I believed I had changed the course of my family's legacy. I believed I had planted myself in a garden of eternal life, prosperity and truth. A garden that anyone would be blessed to be a part of, that no one would ever want to leave. After all, when you're given the fullness of truth and everything you'd ever need to survive, why would you leave it?

But what I didn't know was that I was about to learn that the truth of another person's soul can be vastly different than my own. So much so, that right from the start I was going to come to terms with a fruit of my own making, ripping himself from my garden bed.

On the day my son Beckham was born, and I held him in my arms for the first time, I breathed him in and nuzzled his sweet wet nose against mine.

"Hello," I had said. "I'm your Mommy."

His wails quieted and he opened his eyes in response. We laid there staring at each other taking it all in. This new sacredness. This fresh existence—like nothing had ever existed until this moment. As I held his tiny bundled body in my arms, a soft whisper swept over me.

"He will never serve a mission," the whisper had said.

Knowing that every Mormon male is expected to serve a two-year mission, this statement was… profound. My own husband, my son's father, didn't serve a mission and was constantly questioned about it—the quiet judgement from others had been deafening.

If Beckham never served a mission, it didn't matter—not to me. Even back then. But I was fearful for how the church would treat him. How his friends' opinions of him might change. How he would be viewed negatively by people that were supposed to love him. I had held his tiny infant body tighter against mine that day. With tears in my eyes and his body safe in my arms, I smiled and thought, "you will be whoever you want to be."

It was then that I knew Beckham was not meant to be planted in the same garden bed I had planted myself into. He simply decided this only moments after exiting the womb. It was as if his soul had spoken to mine, letting me know that he was not meant to be contained any longer. I may have made his body but his soul was not of my making.

As his mom, my duty was not to force my ideals of garden life on him, but to love him unconditionally as he journeyed into a joyful existence all his own. As he fulfilled his soul's greatest desires.

A year went by, and I had stayed in my garden bed but never forgot the voice that spoke to me the day Beckham was born. Then one Sunday, fresh out of the shower but dressed for church I went downstairs to discover Travis sitting on the couch in his sweats watching football.

"Are you going to get ready? We need to leave for church soon," I had said. He looked at the ground.

"I need a break."

"What?" I asked, confused. I felt my brow furrow.

"I need a break from church," he said. "Like a long break. I don't think I want to go anymore."

A wave of relief washed over me, which was really confusing. Then it was followed by a wave of guilt and an even bigger wave of panic.

"Okayyyy," I said slowly.

Then I turned and walked back up the stairs and into our bedroom. I quietly closed the door and sat on the floor like I always did when I needed a good cry. Once those floodgates opened, my emotions became indecipherable. My thoughts began to race. My heart pounded in my ears. My body reacted by sweating and shaking. It was a fight or flight moment for me.

My husband had left our garden box.

The box that kept us safe. The box that kept us together forever. The box that held the soil that fed us and was supposed to help us grow into our potential. For some reason his desertion of our garden box felt different than the knowing in my heart that Beckham would need to be planted elsewhere. His leaving almost felt like betrayal. Certain death—of our family, of us, of our eternity together.

It felt like a deep, fatal stab in the heart.

But privately in those moments, I couldn't help but wonder why I had quietly made peace with Beckham leaving our garden bed, but when Travis wanted to leave I felt heartbroken, terrified and helpless. And at the same time, it was like I'd been given permission to finally open the cage I had placed myself in.

I have since come to realize that the love I have for my husband is very different than the love I have for my child. Both are unconditional, but one is chosen and the other is a part of me. My child and I are connected on a cellular level. It's such a foundational love that it's instinctual. And nothing could change the love that exists there. Especially not a religious organization— one that teaches families are forever, at that. I felt on a soul level if anyone understood that concept, it would be God himself.

And yet, during that time of transitioning for our family, my thoughts had been everywhere.

Do I stay in my garden bed alone?

Why did it feel so good when he had said he wanted to leave?

If I stayed, will we be at odds over religious views?

Was our marriage over?

What will it do to Beckham?

If I didn't believe in Mormonism, what did I believe in?

Were we bad?

Would we be denied our eternity together?

I felt so guilty that a part of me was relieved.

I was finally free.

No one could know.

We would lose their respect.

No one would love me anymore.

I didn't stop crying for weeks.

The months following were a blur. My face was constantly wet from tears, and I was on my knees in prayer more than I'd ever been.

I was angry. I was broken. I was lost. I was incredibly scared.

It was like Travis had challenged me to my roots. He had ripped his own roots out of a life that no longer suited his growth. And he was happy. I was jealous that it was so easy for him. I was angry that he seemed so resolute and content with his decision—able to leave it all behind, risking our forever family, and yet I was drowning in the trenches, grasping for anything stable and lifesaving to hold onto.

I wanted to be happy too, but I didn't know how. Unlike Travis, my entire identity had been reliant on the teachings of Mormonism.

I started writing, praying and reading—trying to make sense of it all.

I had felt myself spiraling.

Cracking.

Shifting.

It was truly the most devastating thing I had yet to experience in my young life. And looking back, everything I was programmed to be had begun malfunctioning. Wires were crossing, lighting up my brain and sending my body into panic.

The thing about leaving an orthodox religion is that you are conditioned to believe there is no other option for you outside the safety of your celestial garden box. If you choose to leave, you've made a dire mistake—one that will have eternal consequences. You are programmed to believe that you cannot feel true joy without them. You're made to believe that your purpose lies within the church and cannot be fulfilled without it. And when all that fails to keep you, they remind you that you will be sacrificing eternity with your family if you leave. That if there is an afterlife, they won't be in it. You will be alone forever.

Simply put, you are planted in the garden bed next to everyone else. Then given the exact same things you need to presumably survive.

But what if we humans, who on a cellular level need all of the *same* things to survive and flourish, who are of the *same* species, who can all do great and wonderful things if they are given the right amounts of nourishment, are one and the same with these veggies? What if just like a vegetable garden we all must be strategically placed next to other plants that give us nourishment and kept away from others who stunt our growth? What if we all need the same basic things to survive, but unique and individual nourishments to *thrive*?

It would take me years to understand how to grow as an individual without the church. Before that could happen, I had to go on a journey all my own. I had to let parts of me wilt and die, while new growth took place in other areas.

109

Two years after that pivotal Sunday morning, I fully resigned from the church. I didn't resign because Travis left. I didn't resign because I wanted to sin freely. I didn't resign because I wasn't a faithful member. I resigned because for the first time I let my inner child speak to me. I resigned because the church had served its purpose in my life, the purpose of giving me the family I didn't have but always wanted. The family that is healthy, whole and all encompassing. The family that would not abandon me, lie to me, or pretend to be happy.

I realized through my faith transition that the real reason I joined the church all those years ago was because the idea of a healthy family appealed to me—and now I have it. And nothing else was true to me anymore. I signed away my "eternity" to follow my own truth, my own heart, and to save the family I created. In the church's eyes, by signing the document I had signed away eternity with my husband and son. With a flick of a pen, the Church of Jesus Christ of Latter-Day Saints no longer believed our family would be together forever. It was done. I had officially uprooted myself and embarked on a new journey. I did it quietly, privately and in a way that made me feel safe.

That is when I began to realize that I am a pepper, bold with flavor, bright in appearance, and full of essential purpose, but was in a toxic garden bed that left me dull, small and incapable of reaching my full potential. And although it served a purpose at one time, I had outgrown that garden bed in many ways.

Through my deconstruction, I understood that I was planted beside people that were quite literally adding poison to the soil. My roots retracted and I no longer felt safe in my environment. I learned the history of how my garden bed was built, and the hidden truths behind the foundation. I learned that the organization I had dedicated my life to had manipulated, molded and conditioned me to become a different type of veggie than I was meant to be.

On the outside I seemed to be happy, thriving and rooted. I served in high callings within the women's organization, bore my testimony of the gospel whenever I could, and for a period was attending the temple weekly on top of my commitment to attending church on Sunday for three hours and dedicating my time to finishing my bachelor's degree.

I had a lot on my plate, but God always came first. And yet, on the inside I was slowly dying.

My roots shriveled and died. My life purpose had become to keep everyone around me comfortable. Disappoint no one except myself. Ask questions but never challenge the order of things. Submit to the patriarchy and be a dutiful woman—seen, but not heard. Stay small. Stay obedient. Stay likeable.

While the initial shock was incredibly painful, even after a few weeks I began to enjoy the freedom to explore life. I began to see the world differently. I began to see the church differently. I tried to replant myself multiple times in different garden beds, but nothing felt right. I began to open up to family and friends about my departure and the differences in our relationships were instantly palpable.

The fact is, not all people are meant to be planted in the same soil as me. Not everyone is meant to grow alongside me in happy unison. In order for me to grow big and tall and be everything I am meant to be, I had to take control of who I plant beside myself and in what garden box I plant myself in. The toxic brussels sprout in my life—maybe it was a parent, a friend, a coworker or some other person that was sucking me dry—had to be ripped out of my garden. I had to plant them in another garden bed before learning how to grow fiercely and ferociously and powerfully in my space next to people that gave me nourishment. People who I nourished back with just my existence alone.

It is possible to love something from afar. I didn't have to rip all of the other veggies out, ignore them and let them die. It's called healthy boundaries. My boundary is my garden bed. Inside of my garden, it is full of everything I need to keep growing and thriving. Outside of my garden bed is everything else. The everything else is not up to me and it is not for me. I can still admire it from afar. But I don't live in the "everything else," I live in *my* garden bed.

The "everything else" isn't bad, and the plants that grow there aren't terrible, in fact, they are beautiful in their own way and contribute many great things to the world. But they are not suitable to live in my space, and frankly, I am not suitable to live in theirs—it's a two-way street. Neither of us is better than the other, we are just simply incompatible to live in the same garden bed. It's really about being true to myself and acknowledging what is best for me in order to genuinely thrive.

I think many of us tend to put this very concept on the back burner in an attempt to create harmony in a relationship. We are so attached to this idea of what we want the relationship to look like that we sacrifice what we need to stay connected to that fantasy. But what we don't see is the fantasy itself—the make-believe. It's not a bad thing to want our fantasies to become reality, but it is full self-sabotage when we deny ourselves the things we need to truly thrive for something that is toxic. And while planting ourselves in a new garden bed may seem scary and painful (which it is), what's scarier and more painful is allowing ourselves to be sucked dry by people or an institution that is supposed to love us and leave us thriving.

What's scarier is denying ourselves true happiness to make everyone else happy. What's more painful is knowingly wilting and dying for another that wouldn't do the same for us.

And so, I ask you this. Who would you be if no one else had a say in your destiny? If disappointment wasn't an issue? If love wasn't conditional?

Just who would *you* be?

What would *you* do?

Where would *you* go?

The answers? Anything.

Everything.

Anywhere.

permission

If you have to ask for permission
to live life on your terms, that is not love,
that is control.

"You are so brave!" a voice behind me had said.

I turned to see a woman, around the same age as me. Her hair was long and brunette. Her porcelain skin was young and flawless. She had a slender build with delicate feminine features. It was Sunday so it didn't surprise me to see her dressed in a long skirt and blouse. I smiled back at her, but a look of confusion must have crossed my face because she laughed and started to explain.

"I noticed that you cut your hair. I could never do that. And even if I wanted to, my husband would *never* let me." She laughed and touched my arm in a lighthearted way. "Maybe someday I can be like you. Brave," she said, before smiling and walking away.

I stood there alone for what seemed like an eternity, but it was only a moment. People walked past me to their Sunday school classes. The hallway was buzzing with chatter. I clutched my scriptures to my chest with such force I heard the delicate paper crinkle beneath the weight of my arms. It was a moment of reckoning between Eunice and her own soul that she'd locked away so long ago.

My husband walked up behind me and gently touched my arm.

"You ready to go to class?" he asked as he took a few steps forward. I stood solid as a statue. I didn't answer him.

"That woman just told me I was brave for cutting my hair. Isn't that weird?" Travis opened his mouth to answer but I cut him off.

"Then she said her husband would never *let her* cut her hair." My voice got louder. "But it's *her* hair!" I felt myself getting warm and made an effort to quiet my voice. People had begun to stare.

"Right before she walked away, she said she hoped she could be brave like me someday. All I did was cut my hair. That's not brave."

"But to her you are," Travis said, in his usual calm and assured manner.

Perspective.

I sighed and looked at the ground, annoyed and shaking my head.

"I guess so…"

We went to Sunday school, and I opened my scriptures and pretended to be engaged for the entire hour. But inside, Eunice had cracked open the vault door to her soul and she began to think. Hard.

Back to the time in high school when I was scared of love. It was big and real and all encompassing. He was my friend first, and unexpectedly became my boyfriend. And as all LDS men are expected to do, he put his papers in to serve a mission. Immediately after graduating from high school, he put on a suit and tie and a black embossed name tag to fly wherever the church sent him. And for two years, the only way I could communicate with him was by writing letters or emailing. During that time, I'd started college, was meeting new people, and had also begun planning for the next steps in my life.

116

I had been encouraged to stop being a distraction to him, so he could serve the Lord without being lovesick for a girl back home. I didn't want to but felt like I had to. I had thought breaking up with him was the noble thing to do. But it turned out, it was the first time I experienced true, overwhelming heartbreak. I chose God and the church over love, and even though I internally suffered for months at a love lost, I felt brave for making such a righteous, bold decision.

I thought back graduating from high school and moving 600 miles away to a place I'd never been to go to college. I had applied to live in an apartment full of girls I'd never met, in an apartment I'd never seen. I thought back to move-in day, when my mom left crying and I had spread my wings to start a new chapter of my life without giving it a second thought. She hadn't wanted me to go so far away, and if it were up to her I'm sure she would've chosen a college much closer to home. But that wasn't what I had wanted. I remembered the first day of classes, showing up early and taking my seat in the front row of each class. I had known no one. I lived with strangers. I had had $100 dollars in my bank account and no job.

Was I nervous? Yes! But did I let that stop me? Hell no.

I felt brave then too.

During my freshman year in college I joined a group of people I'd never met to go ice climbing in Bozeman, Montana. We'd met in a dark parking lot before the sun rose, all my gear was in my pack and I was ready to go on an adventure—one I'd never attempted nor researched much about. We drove for hours before finally arriving at the discreetly marked, snow-packed trailhead in rural Montana. We snowshoed three miles uphill before reaching the falls, which was a 200-foot sheer cliff-face made of solid ice. On that trip, I learned the basics of ice climbing,

117

belay tactics and how to pee in the woods with layers of snow gear on. I was terrified of heights but pushed myself up the cliff-face anyway using nothing but my ice axe, crampons and sheer strength—which I found I didn't have much of. I was proud to have done that without the comfort of a friend. I had gone out on my own to explore something I had found interesting.

I didn't ask permission. I didn't want anyone's approval. I just wanted to live. Explore. Thrive. Did I feel a little inadequate, doing something new without knowing much about it? Absolutely! Was I a little shy at first to meet new people and commit to a somewhat extreme adventure with them? Yes, understandably so!

To me, *that* was brave.

Cutting my hair? Not so much.

It sounds silly, but for years this conversation has haunted me. Sometimes I wish I could go back and say just the right thing to her—the girl who wanted to be brave. I wanted to smile at her the way she had smiled at me and say, "What does it mean to be brave? And what things in your life keep you from being brave? Why do you ask for permission to do things that make you happy?"

I also wanted to explain to her that being brave is not extraordinary. At least not to me. Being brave is probably the most ordinary thing ever. That is because being brave is not always a choice—sometimes it's an act of survival and other times we don't even recognize it within ourselves until someone else points it out. Sometimes being brave is the difference between surviving and thriving.

Being brave is not this unachievable, untouchable thing. Being brave equates to just living. Being brave is giving yourself permission to live life on your terms—living in a way that makes you feel happy and strong and joyful. Being brave is simply experiencing life to the fullest extent, without waiting around for approval, permission and sometimes for someone else's company.

It is the art of being true to yourself even if it means disappointing people you love. It is the practice of authentic awareness of self. Bravery is the verb of living a true life. What's beautiful about that is the definition of bravery is as unique as we are. It is a currency that will never depreciate. It holds the same value in each person.

As a woman, bravery is especially powerful. Being a brave woman means that I actively outgrow every toxic box and mold that I've been shaped and carved and shoved into from the time I was a little girl. Being a brave woman means that I no longer forsake myself just so people will like me. Being a brave woman means that I don't make myself smaller just to make others comfortable. Being a brave woman means rejecting the idea that in order to be good, I have to be perfect. Being brave means I accept myself as I am and live as authentically as possible.

We need to start unwrapping bravery from its gilded wrapper. It is not a Wonka Bar. There is no golden ticket of bravery that one gets lucky with. It is not a gift that some are born with and others are not.

Bravery lies within choice. A choice to live an authentic life without asking for permission.

Bravery lies within giving yourself permission to be whoever the hell you want to be. Not just permission to go out and do great and wonderful and powerful things. No. Permission to just *be*.

Glennon Doyle says, *To be brave is to forsake all others to be true to yourself.* Why is this so hard for women? Why can't we just be true to ourselves? Why is it considered brave for a woman to give herself permission to forsake all others?

Why is it brave to cut your hair?

Because as women, we've been conditioned since the days of Eve to make everyone else around us comfortable and happy. We've been taught that if we slip up and take others down the rabbit hole with us, it leads to eternal damnation for the rest of humanity. Taking a bite of the apple means being cast out, deemed unworthy, falling out of favor.

To that I raise my glass and say, take a bite out of the damn apple!

You will never truly live if you are constantly asking for permission. You will never show your children what it's like to take a risk and succeed or fail and rise up again. You will never explore your soul if you keep asking everyone else around you what's right and what's wrong. You will never develop your own sense of identity if you keep asking others for approval of your choices or permission to live a life that brings you joy.

If you have to ask for permission to live life on your terms, that is not love, that is control.

Let me ask you this… if those around you cast you out and deem you unworthy, did they love you to begin with? Or was their love conditional based on submission and their own ideals of how you should live your life? If they cast you out and deem you unworthy, is it in the name of God or is it based on their own human construct of meeting certain requirements to be worthy of love?

If it is, it's most likely because they are trapped in the same god-forsaken mess you're trapped in. They are living their life holding fast to the iron rod of conditions, expectations and complete control because they too know what will happen if they let go. If they have just a taste of that apple. They know, but they won't say it.

So let them cast you out. Let them deem you unworthy. Let them talk about you behind your back and pray for you at night. Let them create their own version of you in their minds—after all, none of that is up to you anyway. Just as your life was never in their hands in the first place. The church made you think it was, but it wasn't. Your life has always been yours. The tether was never tied. The door has always been open.

The apple has always been in your hand.

Like a bird born in a cage, you've never stretched your wings to fly freely through the wind, taken a deep dive into the depths of the sea or tasted the wildness the earth has to offer. You've sat perfectly still on your perch, singing the songs you were taught to sing, and never questioning the cage you sat inside day after day. Taking flight will feel... weird, awkward, messy and clumsy. But it will also feel exciting, joyful, relieving and truthful.

If you leave the church or if you already have, my advice to you is to give yourself permission to feel all the feelings. You don't need to feel guilty anymore. You don't need to question yourself or your emotions. Sit with yourself, be gentle. Cry, journal, read, listen to podcasts, go to therapy—whatever it is that you need to do, do it.

And don't ask for permission.

Remember that if you are the hottest mess this earth has ever seen, that's okay. Be that mess. Give yourself permission to be messy. I always have to remind myself that I don't live in the mess—I visit the mess. The mess is not permanent. Remember that. Being brave is allowing yourself to visit the mess, stay there a while, rest up, and then rise.

Greatness does not lie in the mess. It lies in the shattered glass on the floor that you must walk over with bare feet to move forward from the mess.

As Glennon Doyle says, *Be messy and complicated and afraid, and show up anyway*. That is brave. Showing up, messy, complicated, afraid, broken, frustrated, with permission from yourself.

Brave.

indoctrinated

*"Be prayerful and be consistent in your study of the scriptures
that you may be prepared in the responsibilities you will have.
You will at times have the ability to recall the things that are
important as you help others understand their life and the things
that are important. It is important that you keep a journal, that
you have a record that will be acceptable to the Lord concerning
the things that occur in your life. Your Heavenly Father has
promised you that through your faithfulness you will come forth
in the morning of the first resurrection to enjoy eternal life."*

Patriarchal Blessing of Lindsay Helm

Dear Diary,

*Life is going much better. I feel more receptive to the
spirit and less foggy brained. I need to do better at having an
attitude of gratitude. I love the restored gospel and I need to take
time to read my scriptures and ponder every day.*

*I am doing this program called "Get Connected" on
campus. It is a program that uses volunteers to help out incoming
freshman. I was selected to be an ITEAM LEADER (group
leader). I will be over a group of 15-25 new students.*

*This weekend we had a training for it. The correct term
was Spirit Conference. During Spirit Conference we had a spirit
challenge where we were blindfolded and led through the snow
out into a field somewhere and left there alone. Loud music was
playing over speakers placed throughout the field, we were
supposed to find the prophet's voice amidst the chaos. There were
people role-playing the "spirit" and other people role-playing the
"devils." The spirits (Holy Ghost) whispered quietly around me*

and kept their distance. I could barely hear them above the music. The devils spoke loudly—basically shouting, and they were physically touching me. They walked next to me shouting, making it hard to follow the quiet promptings of the spirits.

Eventually, after listening carefully to the spirits, I found the prophet's voice after wandering through the snow for a while. Soon enough, I found the iron rod, which was a long rope leading up what seemed like a steep embankment. I held it as I followed it up this mountain where people were singing hymns. When I got up to the top and took off my blindfold, I saw familiar faces and it was like a small glimpse of heaven. It was amazing.

I am so happy that I have the opportunity to be with my loved ones again. I can't wait to be free of worry, doubt and temptation. I can't wait for absolute peace.

I've often been asked, "How could you believe all that stuff? How could you allow yourself to be so... controlled?"

The thing about mind control is that it happens subtly and over time. Becoming Eunice began the moment I was baptized. Day by day, minute by minute. Being 13 when I joined the church made me very malleable, soft and easy to manipulate.

By the time I was 19 years old, living in Rexburg and attending BYU-I, I was all in. I was on the fast track to what I believed to be eternity. My blinders were on. So much so that I actually thought this experience of being blindfolded and left outside in the east Idaho snow was profound. Looking back, it was a cosplay on my psyche. It was furthering my mind control as I was forced to act out my journey to heaven.

The journey to righteousness.

The journey to enduring to the end.

One wrong step, one wrong voice listened to, and I would be led astray from the group. Out into the frozen field on my own, which would've been a metaphorical "outer darkness" or hell.

I was only 19 the day I was left in the snow with spirits and devils played by my peers. The day I was trying to make it to heaven by choosing the right. The day when grown adults in the church put together this activity and thought it was completely harmless. In fact, they thought it was the opposite. They thought it was heavenly, wholesome and beautiful. Because they too had been subjected to activities like this. They too, were controlled.

They say that, typically, the abused can likely become the abusers. It's a vicious cycle. High demand religion is no different. The manipulated become the manipulators. The controlled become the controllers. The power moves from one generation, to the next, until an army of indoctrinated young humans march to the orders of their leaders, blindfolded, in a snowy field on a Saturday.

Since leaving the church, a big part of my healing process has been going back into my journals and reading about my experiences and reflecting on the level of indoctrination I was subjected to. Sometimes I notice a common theme in those passages. A sense of despair emerges. And what follows is a sense of inner conflict and a sense of being out of control, while manically trying to maintain control and not realizing I was in fact being controlled. It was like I was in a constant state of panic and anxiety, always wondering if I was good enough. Wondering if I would make it to heaven or if I was worthy of God's love.

The following journal passages were written while attending my freshman and sophomore years in college:

Dear Diary,

My heart is full today. I've just re-read my patriarchal blessing. I've read about the woman I am to become. I understand now that my blessings will only be granted based on my obedience to the commandments and fulfilling my divine responsibilities. I don't know what my divine responsibilities are yet. I desperately wish to know. But everything will be revealed in the Lord's time. I hope I will fulfill my divine responsibilities to my Heavenly Father's expectations. I am striving to be a righteous daughter of God. I hope I am doing good enough. I know I can always do better.

Every time I feel stressed, I remember what it says in my patriarchal blessing. It says I will have the help of heaven in all I undertake. That always helps me feel better. I love my Heavenly Father. I feel like something big is coming, but I don't know what. God has big plans for me, I can feel it. I hope I am ready.

Dear Diary,

I am so thankful for the knowledge of my Heavenly Father. I am so happy to know that He has a plan for me. I want to devote my entire life, soul and body to do the work He needs me to do. I know I am here for a reason. I know I am here to learn and grow. In my patriarchal blessing, it says that I am a chosen daughter. I have always felt special, like I have something important to do with my life. I can't do it without Heavenly Father's help. I love Him so much. I am awful at praying. I feel my spirit wrestle within me when it is spiritually malnourished. I can do better. I need to do better. I won't make it if I don't. I need to do better, not only for my sake but for Travis as well. We need each other to be spiritually strong. We have important work to do. We must be ready to be a tool in the Lord's hands at any time. I hope I live my life to the satisfaction of my Father in Heaven. I hope I pass the test of life. I want to be a person that makes Satan tremble. He won't ever win. He will never have me. I'm on the Lord's side and He will always prevail.

Dear Diary,

I am not very good at praying. I want my relationship with God to be good and strong. I'm reading my scriptures and I have tried to say more meaningful prayers. I just feel like God isn't pleased with me. I'm trying so hard to be good, obedient and righteous. I've even started listening to church music in my car instead of the radio. I feel like I've changed some. I want to be sweeter, kinder and more charitable. Maybe I need to do more service. I feel overwhelmed. I want my Father in Heaven to be proud of me.

The journaling I did, and still do, spans hundreds of pages, and multiple books. The further I go back, the more painful it is to read.

I wish I could go back in time, find my younger self, and give her a big hug. I would tell her that I love her, that she is good enough, and that God and the universe and the "something bigger" love her beyond words. She doesn't need to prove it and she never had to. Her worth has always been inherent. She doesn't need to have all the answers. I would also tell her to trust herself more. I would tell her to rip off the blindfold and make her own path up the fucking mountain. Or anywhere she pleases. Even when the people around her would gawk and stare, wondering what she was doing, I would tell her to pay no mind to them. I would tell her that it will be scary and unknown and lonely at times, but everything would be worth it. I would tell her that the people close to her would rally and love and support her no matter what. And no matter what, she was doing good enough. Always.

After all, her strength was always within her, but the church convinced her that it was safer to trust them than it was to trust herself. Because the church was God's church and could never be swayed by Satan. But us humans? We were just a "natural man" easily tempted by the Adversary. We could not be trusted. Not without them. Not without the church. However, the monster that lurks in the water of my subconscious is the control the church had over me.

Sometimes, I crave that control. Like a drug, the control lurks in muddy water, calling my name. It asks me to let it back in, just for a moment. And like that monster, it opens its jaws and waits. It waits until I am vulnerable and then it strikes. But before that happens, the victim, the addict within me, craves the control— because control is safety. Control makes me feel like my life has a finite path that is less scary than freedom. Control is the path to goodness, the iron rod, salvation, eternal life. Control is all I know. And when I feel a lack of control, I notice flare ups of certain behaviors.

Behaviors like possessiveness, isolation, the need to control insignificant things in my life, extreme stubbornness, and being unwilling to compromise. Because everything in my life for 10 years was highly controlled, sometimes a lack of control leaves me floundering. But I always bring myself back to those journal entries. I remind myself of a time when I was being controlled but I, myself, had no actual control. While I was in the church I didn't perceive it that way, but now being on the outside I can see it for what it really is. And I know that I never actually had any semblance of control over my life.

How could I when everything was decided for me?

As a person who experiences religious trauma, I often have nightmares. I've found a pattern to them. Many of them revolve around losing control, screwing up my life and being sorely misunderstood.

On one such occasion, I woke up and journaled about it:

Dear Diary,

Last night, I woke up from a dream that made me feel like I had just taken 12 steps backward. I woke up sweaty and unsure. I wasn't sure if it was a dream or reality at first, and my anxiety was heightened. But after a few seconds, I realized I was safe in my warm bed, next to my snoring husband with my fluffy Siamese snuggled between my feet. I laid back down and immediately found refuge in deep sleep.

But this morning, I was haunted by it.

In my dream I was starting a new job as a school bus driver in my hometown, Richland. On my first day, without any training, they gave me a piece of paper with my route on it. I was panicking but had confidence I could figure it out—and also didn't want to make a fuss. I went on my way, started my bus and began my route. I found my first stop no problem. But the illusive second stop was nowhere to be found. I felt myself start to panic thinking of those kids standing outside in the cold waiting for their bus that would never come. For some reason, I didn't think to call for help, I just kept going. Ultimately, I decided the map had to be wrong, so I decided to help out one of my fellow bus drivers who had too many kids for his bus. I offered to take some of them in my bus since we were going to the same place. They gladly hopped in my bus and away we went.

As I was driving down a road I have been down a million times, the road began to change. Suddenly, the road was not familiar anymore. The exits, highway ramps and roundabouts all morphed before my eyes. Thick, black grates rose out of the concrete between the lanes so cars could not change lanes at all. It created a small barrier between lanes that would definitely damage a car if they tried to go over them.

Panicking, I maneuvered the bus as well as I could, but was going too fast and didn't know which way to go. Nothing looked familiar and the grates were controlling which way I could drive. I tried my best to decipher the new routes and road signs. I tried to change lanes several times, but the grates prevented me from doing so. The wheels were grinding against the grates— metal on metal, sparks flying, bus jolting violently.

After multiple attempts, I finally jumped the bus over the grates to take the exit that I thought would take us to the school, but instead it ended up leading us in the direction of a neighboring town in the opposite direction. Everyone aboard the bus moaned and groaned—I was letting them down. I wasn't doing good enough. A driver should always know where to go.

I tried to remain positive and said things like "well guys we are taking the scenic route to school today!" and "It's okay! We will get there eventually! Just means less school for you!" No one was impressed. They were all inconvenienced and it was my fault. The energy in the bus was somber—angry even. And it was all because of me.

As we made our way down the highway, toward another town, I attempted to put my cruise control on, but the moment I pushed the button on the steering wheel, the bus became a super speed death mobile that was flying over 85mph on the highway. The bus was going so fast, everything outside its windows became a blur. My hands turned white as I held the steering wheel as tight as I could. Through gritted teeth I tried to maintain control of the bus, but the faster we went the more squirrelly the bus became. No matter what I did, I couldn't slow the bus down. I had to maneuver the bus through lanes of traffic, trying not to hit other cars. Meanwhile, the roadside speed gauges were snapping pictures of me every mile. I was going at least 20mph over the speed limit. I was definitely going to get a ticket. My blood was boiling with panic. I have completely lost control and there is nothing I can do. The kids in my bus were starting to get scared and told me to slow down, but I couldn't.

After what seemed like several panic inducing minutes, with all my strength I pushed the brake to the floor. Even that didn't make the bus stop, but it slowed it down. I kept pumping the break all the way to the floor, and eventually we slowed down enough to find our exit just in time, and eventually we made it to our destination.

I woke up sweaty, sick to my stomach, head throbbing. My tear-stained pillow showed the evidence of my panic.

After my morning coffee, I had time to think about what this dream meant. It was obvious that it had something to do with control.

The part about self-preservation that I have learned over time is its insatiable need for control. Self-preservation is about survival. And survival is about learning where you are safe and where you are not. And if you can manipulate your world to always feel safe, that is control.

I never thought of myself as a blatantly controlling person, but as I grew into myself and began to understand this thing called self-preservation, I began to notice some of my own controlling tendencies. This dream in particular, reminded me that I have a lot of work left to do.

A question I have is, why is control so comforting? And why does the lack of control leave me feeling like I need a nap?

I became acutely aware of what my dream was telling me: In order to save yourself and everyone else on this bus, you need to maintain control. If you lose control, everyone will "die" and it will be your fault. Even though the bus company didn't train you properly and even though the roads were morphing like some kind of fucked up horror film, it will all be your fault. You should be able to control the uncontrollable. You should be able to keep everyone comfortable in the back of the bus even in the midst of certain death. Keep them happy and keep smiling so they don't sense your discomfort, keep playing the part of driver, that's your job. It is up to you, and you alone.

This dream still haunts me. Feeling out of control was absolutely terrifying.

The truth is, I was never in control and was spiraling for years to try and maintain what control I thought I had. The level of indoctrination I had endured, trained me to believe that the world outside of the church was dangerous and should not be trusted. It trained me to believe that they had all the answers and their rules kept me safe—they kept me on the straight and narrow path toward celestial glory. And if I "jumped the grates" so to speak and left the preordained lane I was expected to stay in, I would be lost, out of control, and speeding toward failure.

It's been over six years since I left the church and I still feel the lack of control, but not *out of control*. I have moments where there is an illusion of being out of control, but it is just that—an illusion. It is my trauma speaking, but it is not truth. The truth is, at this point in my life, I feel grounded, rooted, yet simultaneously free. I feel like at any moment, I could float away on a billowing current of whatever is meant for me—and I wouldn't fight it. I would let it take me to the next great and wonderful thing that awaits. I have ownership over my own life, and I take responsibility for the things that happen within it. My trauma responses tell me that I won't be okay in an uncontrolled environment, but my soul tells me that I am good, I am loved and I am safe. I trust her—my soul—completely.

Healing takes time, and some days I wonder why it's taken this long to heal as much as I have. But when I look back on how far I've come, I begin to understand. Healing is not a linear journey. Sometimes it looks more like a mountaineering expedition or swimming in circles, but progress is progress.

Now, six years later, I look toward the sky with open arms, floating weightlessly on the waves of intent, trust and something bigger than me. I've come to the realization that the only thing in my control is my refusal to drown.

My refusal to give up.

gone

Dying of a broken heart certainly sounds poetic. Romantic. Shakespearian even. Until it's not.

Sometimes it is the belief that no one would care if you were suddenly gone. That is the thought that, for a split second, had dug its claws into my soul.

No one would care if I was gone.

No one would care.

No one.

Gone.

Trembling, I had reached toward the cupboard under the sink. The red and black handles of the scissors had stared at me. I felt their weight, the coldness of the metal, the sharp tips of each blade.

When I opened them, they made the distinct swishing sound of metal against metal. Like sharpening a knife, the way my grandpa used to on Thanksgiving right before carving the turkey.

I laid the open blades gently on my bare thigh. The cold metal had felt so good. Tears streamed down my face and dripped onto my warm skin below. My thighs were splattered and salty. My heart quickened its pace.

This wasn't me.

I retraced my memories back to a time when I had felt like everyone loved me. When I was praised for being so happy, diligent and a good example to other young women. When I was surrounded by friends everywhere I went. When I blindly followed orders, I had been gifted the magic ticket of instant friendship.

But that late evening, I had felt alone.

I remembered a time when the only credential I needed to have love in my life was showing up to church, doing church things, and "staying in line."

But a part of staying in line was doing my "duty" as a woman. Get married and have babies. But I wasn't ready, and I had hated them for that—the church. I hated them for pressuring me into adulthood too fast. Nineteen wasn't old enough to get married. Ten months married before having a baby wasn't long enough. Twenty-two came too fast. The young girl inside me grieved, not having these experiences on my own time. The experience of dating my soulmate and marrying him, on my time. And the experience of meeting my other soulmate, our son, on my time.

Not theirs.

I hated them for forcing me to grow up too fast. I hated them for taking my independence from me. I hated them for conditioning me to need the checklists, the perfection, and the accolades. It was like a drug. The toxic perfectionism is all I knew.

Without it, I was lost.

Without the checklists and control and everyone's eyes watching at all times, I didn't know how to behave. I didn't know what was true and what was fake. I didn't know what was real and what was made-up. I didn't know what was genuine and what was a lie.

And now I was screwing everything up.

My husband was 800 miles away finishing his master's degree—something else the church had encouraged us to do. As a man, Travis' job was to take care of us. To provide for us. And mine was to be there waiting for him. To take care of our son. To keep having babies and be a meek and mild housewife. To be trapped inside a life I wasn't ready for.

But what about me? What about us?

Travis was supposed to come home months ago, but he hadn't. He had said it was because of his research. But I thought he was leaving me.

I thought he was leaving us.

My thoughts raced rapidly, out of control. My son would be awake soon. No one cared. Everyone hated me. I was a burden on every single person I knew. I knew they talked about me when I left the room. Travis wanted to leave me. He wished he never married me. No one cared. My existence didn't matter. They never liked me. I was a shitty mom and everyone knew it. I was so lonely. And I was angry that I couldn't be better.

Why couldn't I be better?

I sobbed through gritted teeth and pressed the blade harder against my thigh.

Harder.

Harder.

Harder.

Pain shot up the inside of my leg and it had felt so good. My cries had turned into sobs and my sobs turned into the manic gasps of an injured soul. I held the scissors there for a few moments before I realized what I was doing.

I threw the scissors across the bathroom and stood to look at myself in the mirror. I steadied myself on the bathroom sink, as

I had felt weak with grief. Through blurred vision I stared at my injured reflection.

"None of that is true!" I sobbed to myself.

A small red line throbbed slightly on the surface of my ivory skin.

I fell to my knees and curled my body as tight as I could between the toilet and sink, staring at the 70s tile I'd attempted to scrub clean over a hundred times. I laid down, still curled up tight, feeling one and the same with the filthy bathroom floor.

"None of that is true," I whispered. "None of that is true. None of that is true."

I closed my eyes and laid still until I stopped sobbing. Then I stayed there, on the cold, grimy bathroom floor where it felt safe and good, and I stared at the ceiling until the tears dried to my face.

"I need help," I had said to myself out loud. "I need help."

It was never my intent to end my life. I'd never wanted that. It was simply that I wanted to inflict all the pain I had been feeling inside, on myself—because I didn't know what else to do. I was inflicting all the pain the church's culture caused me on myself because I hated them, and I hated myself.

I hated them because I blamed them for pressuring Travis and I to get married so young and so fast. I blamed them for our poverty. I blamed them for me being a single mom for almost a year, with no clue what I was doing. I blamed them for pressuring me into motherhood before I was ready. I blamed them for not feeling any sense of control over my life.

Inflicting pain was the one thing I could control. I wanted to hurt myself because I was angry with every cell in my body.

I think back to this young woman and wish I could scoop her up in my arms and hold her. I wish I could have told her, "You are needed on this earth more than you know. You have so much love and beauty and talent and wisdom. You will be okay someday. Better than okay. You will heal and you will move mountains."

It had been two years since we'd left the church. My husband and I had been living apart for almost a year when we'd planned for it to be only a few weeks. We were dirt poor. We had just left a community of people—the church. The church provided built-in friends, a guidebook to life, and resolute direction. And suddenly, that was all gone. I was quite literally alone. Even two years after leaving, I was still going through the deconstruction and deconditioning of the faith I had left. I was like a baby animal learning how to walk for the first time. All while our marriage was on the rocks and I was trying to adapt to being alone while raising a child that I had no clue how to raise.

Even though we had left the church, the residual effects of living in a high control religion still dominated our everyday lives. The decisions we had made while being faithful members of the church still impacted our current lives. On top of it all, I not only lived 800 miles away from Travis, alone with our toddler, but I knew only a handful of people in our new town. I tried to get out of the house, practice self-care, and hold down a small part-time job, but everything had felt impossible. Life was like wading through setting concrete.

What I know now is that I was struggling with depression, although it would not be diagnosed or fully treated for some time. But back then I felt so alone for the first time in my life, and so confused and terribly sad that I truly believed my life meant nothing. And the only thing that felt good was to inflict pain on myself.

Which had terrified me.

A few weeks later I was sitting in a therapist's office, and this time I was nervous. I immediately told her what had happened but left out the part with the scissors. That part scared me so badly, and I didn't trust her yet. I honestly couldn't mutter the words. I was deeply ashamed. I was almost in denial that it even happened. I didn't want it to be true.

There was a part of me that had felt like a failure, which would immediately put a stain on my outward attempt at perfection. I also felt a need to control how other people perceived me—even my therapist. Not only that, but I had wanted to control their emotion, and I knew without a doubt, something that big and potentially life threatening would cause an emotional reaction to any person I told. And I couldn't handle that. And so, with that, I didn't tell her about the scissors. I didn't tell anyone about the scissors, not even Travis.

It became my secret for a few weeks, and then because it was so traumatizing, I buried it. I wouldn't even allow myself to write about it in any way. Not in my journals, not on a scrap piece of paper, not even in the private musings of my mind. So, it stayed buried. And that's where it stayed for many years—buried deep in my subconscious. I never wanted anyone to know because then they'd all know I wasn't perfect. They'd think I was crazy. Maybe they'd even take my son away from me. And what if my disintegrating mental state happened to get back to Mormon friends or family? Would they be so bold to blame it on *me*?

As an active Mormon, I'd often heard the way other members spoke about people who'd left—especially when word spread that the ex-member was going through a hard time. They'd say things like, "This happened to them because God is punishing them for leaving the church and rejecting the gospel. It's because of *their own* disobedience this happened."

As my mind spiraled, once again, I felt it would be *my* fault. I was the broken one. I was the one to blame. I was not good enough. I was the person to point the finger at. It was all on me. From my experience, all the people that used to love me, that used to provide a community for me, would now be comparing my declining mental health to a punishment from God. And once again, the church and its culture would wipe their hands clean and get away scot free. Never taking blame for anything. Never apologizing for damage done.

My new therapist had told me I was very strong and brave to recognize the need for help, following the thoughts I had… in particular the one about no one caring if I was gone. I told her it scared me. It scared me badly, and I never wanted to have that thought again. I told her I knew it wasn't true and couldn't believe I actually had that thought. I almost felt guilty, like somehow it was in my control. But I knew that it wasn't.

This was when I began to recognize that my brain chemistry just wasn't right and my heart shifted. I knew recovery was going to be a long road ahead and that no one else could do it for me. I had to bear down and get it done, no matter how painful. I began to separate the two worlds that for so long had been one, the church's teachings and the worth of my life.

With the recognition that I needed help, somehow, I unlocked the understanding that my soul was not being punished by God. My life was not being plagued with trials and tribulations because I lacked faith. My marriage was not rocky because we broke our temple covenants by withdrawing our church membership. We were simply living. Through the good and the bad. Through the sickness and health. Through the ups and the downs. Through the learning curve of leaving a high control religion and experiencing life anew. And it was then that I became committed to saving my marriage, to saving myself, and to saving my life.

I decided to take back the control I so desperately yearned for. The control I had freely given away. I stood on my own two feet and took a hard look at who I truly was, and who we were as a family. I vowed to never let another organization or person tell me how to live my life again, and I vowed to live for us.

As soon as Travis returned home, I knew we would have work to do. But I knew we could do it. I knew we could redesign our lives to create a cohesive life of our choosing.

torn

Instead of becoming a shiny perfect example,
we leaned into our brokenness and decided
to live our life the best way we knew how.

It had been nearly three months since I hit rock bottom, and Travis was finally on his way home to us. Soon , he'd be driving through the evergreen trees that lined our gravel driveway. Soon I would be able to hear the heavy tires crunch the gravel below. And soon, the love of my life would step out of his car, and we'd finally have the chance to take our lives back—together.

For the first time in nearly a year, both of us would be at the helm of our united ship. We'd be home.

Although we were not entirely established in our newish town, we'd made our rental all our own. Our little home was nestled back in the forest under the shadow of Mt. Rainier. My son and I would often explore the nature outside our front door, and we made many wildlife friends. Deer, opossums, raccoons and even a pack of coyotes graced our steps. Yet, out of all the wildlife to be seen, Beckham loved the slugs, the toads, the gardener snakes and the tree frogs most. Once he even attempted to lick a giant banana slug that he found under a rock. (This is the stuff no one prepares you for. Is there a section in the parent handbook about slug licking? If so, I'd *really* like to read it).

We moved into the little 600-square-foot house, which I nicknamed the Rhododendron House because it sat on a decades' old Rhododendron nursery, when Travis and I had decided to start our postgraduate and post-Mormon lives near his hometown of Buckley, Washington.

We loved the natural beauty of the area and the recreational, educational and career opportunities it provided our family. Housed just one hour from Seattle and less than thirty minutes from Tacoma, with a small town feel and phenomenal views of Mt. Rainier, this place quickly felt like home.

But there had been something missing—Travis. Home didn't feel like home without him.

It was early July by the time Travis made his final trek home—and this time to stay. A few months had gone by since I'd seen him, and during that time he'd finished his master's research and defended his thesis successfully. Our conversations had been brief during that time and usually ended with me in tears. In fact, the last time I had seen him, I thought I was going to die of a broken heart.

He had surprised Beckham and I on a camping trip we took with my mom and stepdad. He drove ten hours just to spend two days with us and had to borrow gas money to get there. I had been prepping the firepit at our campsite when I heard a familiar voice. When our eyes met I was instantly home, even though in reality I was miles away from the Rhododendron House.

Two days later, when it was time to say goodbye, Beckham couldn't understand. He started wailing and trembling and called out for his daddy. Travis and I hugged tighter than we ever have—neither of us wanted to let go. I had felt his heartbeat fast against my chest. I heard his exasperated gasps of a man torn. During the car ride home Beckham had screamed until his tired little body fell asleep. I cried silently until the pain swelled throughout my being. My entire body had felt like it had been hit by a train. I was going home, and yet home couldn't have been farther away.

The day Travis finally did come home, I was anxiously buzzing around the house preparing for his arrival. That evening, I heard the familiar sound of human presence outside the Rhododendron House. Beckham and I excitedly ran to the window. Sure enough, his car was parked right outside.

He was home.

I was home.

We were home!

That night we opened a bottle of port we'd bought months before at a little winery in Leavenworth. We'd been saving it for this day. The day we were together again—for good.

Somehow, we managed to drink the entire bottle in one night. I can't tell you how we did it, but after the first few glasses, everything became a warm, delightful blur.

For the next year, we deconstructed, fought, worked hard, connected, failed and grew. All of our focus was on the three of us—no one else. We became a united, inseparable front. Some of the work was as easy as breathing, but most of the work was like pulling teeth. However, we were committed to starting fresh, taking care of ourselves and each other, and continually moving forward—not just surviving but thriving. But then one day, all of our work, all of our progress, seemed to hit a boiling point.

It was mid-September and we'd decided to do a family fair day at the Washington State Fairgrounds with our brother and sister-in-law, and our nephews and niece. Beckham and my niece were the two littlest ones and couldn't participate in very many things, but the fair still had so much to offer. Food, games, entertainment, and of course, animals.

From the start of the day Travis seemed a bit grumpy, but as the day progressed he completely shut down. He barely spoke, and when he did it was in one-word answers. I kept asking him if he was okay and each time I had been greeted with anger and annoyance as a response. I tried my best to keep a positive attitude and a smile on my face. I didn't want to ruin everyone else's time just because we were struggling through the day.

On the way home, Beckham had fallen asleep in the car and Travis had driven in silence. Because of the anger he'd expressed earlier in the day when I had asked if he was alright, I didn't want to ask again. So, I waited. And waited. And waited. For 20 minutes we drove in complete silence, without even the radio to cut the tension. Without a word, he pulled into the grocery store parking lot next to our house, parked the car, got out and walked away, leaving the car running.

My phone dinged. It was a text from my sister-in-law.

"Is Travis okay?" she asked.

My breath had been caught in my chest as I held back tears. The truth was, this wasn't the first time this had happened since he got home. It was just the first time it had happened in public. There were times where he would just completely shut down and refuse to talk, and everything I said just pissed him off even more. I felt helpless. I wondered what was wrong with *me*. I genuinely wanted to know how he was feeling and if I could help, but I was always met with resistance and anger.

"I'm not sure," I texted my sister-in-law back. "He hasn't spoken to me all day and I don't know why."

I watched as Travis exited the store with a single grocery bag in hand. He opened the driver's side door, got in, and drove us home without speaking a single word.

After we were back home, I immediately went upstairs. I needed to sit on my bedroom floor and think. And cry. I needed to calm myself down before I spiraled into hysteria. I needed to center myself. Something had to change. I was not going to live my life in silence, where speaking about feelings and emotions and helping each other is met with annoyance and hissed remarks. I wanted a marriage that was a partnership. I wanted a marriage where two people could talk about anything and help each other grow. I didn't want this. And truthfully, we had been at this point for some time, but we'd just been good at distracting ourselves.

I wasn't sure how we'd gotten here, and I hadn't wanted to confront it. I hadn't wanted to confront it because… what if they were right? What if everything the church said about leaving was true. That we would never experience true joy again or that God would punish us for breaking our sacred temple covenants? What if my worst fear was about to come true? The fear that without the church our marriage would fail and our family would never be together forever.

Those thoughts along with fear flipped a switch inside of me that day, as I sat on my bedroom floor. I don't know if I was cognitively aware of it at the time but I decided that as an equal partner in this relationship I was going to do something about the situation we had found ourselves in. I was going to stand up for myself. I was going to start a conversation, just as Travis had a few years prior.

The conversation that changed everything.

I wiped my face and stood. I was going to take my power back. I didn't care if Travis got angry or hated me or left—I wasn't going to let this happen to our marriage. To him. To me. To us. I opened the door to our room and walked with purpose to the living room where he sat on the couch watching TV. And I came in hot.

"What is wrong with you?" I asked point blank. He stared at me silently.

"What are you talking about?" he asked. His indifference had annoyed me.

"Don't pretend like nothing is wrong! This is ridiculous. I am not going to live in a house full of silence with people who don't talk to each other! You ignored me all day—gave me the silent treatment, and then you continued it in the car ride home. And any time I asked if you were okay, you were annoyed with me. *Any* time I ask if you are okay when you ignore me you get angry… with *me*! You never want to talk to me and when I try to start a conversation I am basically ignored or given a one-word answer. Sometimes you get angry just because I'm speaking to you! I need to know what's going on. I don't like being ignored. I don't like walking on eggshells. And I feel like I am doing it *all* the time! This is not what I want… I'm done… I'm done."

I couldn't believe I'd just said those words. I'm done? What *was* I done with? Our marriage? His behavior? That argument? All of it? I wasn't sure.

I was proud for not crying while I word-barfed all over him, but the minute I had turned the corner and he was out of sight, I lost it. I cried hysterically. I went to our room and wept on the bed. Then I laid there in silence, tears dried to my face. I had felt like I was losing my best friend all over again. Like my fight to sustain our separation was all for nothing. Like he was here with me, but not really. Like leaving the church had destroyed us. Like getting married so fast while we were so young had destroyed us. Like having a baby so soon had destroyed us. Like living apart for almost a year had destroyed us.

I let my eyes relax as I had come to terms with what I felt like was inevitable. I felt like Travis was unhappy, and like most of the men in my life, he would leave too. And I would blame myself. And, like most of the men in my life, the words "I love you" were always followed with "but…"

I love you, but I can't stay here any longer.

148

I love you, but I can't fight for you.

I love you, but I love myself more.

I love you, but I hate your family.

I love you, but I can't let you in.

I love you, but...

In my hazy state, I saw that a blurred figure had entered the doorway and walked toward the bed. I blinked fast in an effort to focus my vision while I sat up on the bed. In a guttural, heart-wrenching tone I had never heard, Travis stood before me and said, "Something is wrong with me." And burst into tears with so much force it took him to his knees.

The emotion he'd kept inside for so long, found its way out through the wailing of a man who'd suppressed every emotion, opinion and thought for nearly 30 years. As he knelt beside our bed with his head in my lap, I said nothing.

I simply held him.

In the moments after, I rubbed his back and told him how much I'd missed him. How much I loved him. How much I needed him, and how much Beckham needed a father willing to express his emotions in a healthy way.

I told him I'd help him. And that we'd figure this out together.

I held Travis in my arms as his body trembled against mine. His sobs were guttural—like they had been caged inside a wounded soul for far too long. He couldn't speak. But I knew. He needed help too. His arms wrapped around me in a way that felt like he was hanging on for dear life. Like the way you'd hold onto something in fear of falling to your death. Like if you let go, you'd be lost forever. Swept away in your own grief and taken by the demons of a tormented soul.

He'd never held me that way before. This felt different. This felt sacred. This felt like the only true thing in the universe— our bodies together that way. Two injured souls hanging on for dear life, too scared and damaged and broken to let go.

From that moment on, we never let go. In the following weeks, Travis dove deep into his mental and emotional self, and for the first time he admitted that he was experiencing the trauma of believing that as a man his feelings didn't matter. He was deep in a world where emotional connection to anyone and anything seemed impossible. He was so focused on living up to the expectation to provide for his family, that he'd lost himself. And our struggles over the last year were the final nail in his emotional coffin.

Young boys who grow into men with extreme emotional deficits are told to "toughen up," "be a man," "rub some dirt on it," and worst of all, "don't be such a girl."

And men in the LDS culture are given all of that plus the power of the patriarchy. They are taught to use the power of the priesthood (something only righteous LDS males have access to). They are told they are the mouthpiece of God. They are given high responsibility within the church infrastructure, which comes with even more power.

On top of it all, the church culture creates a place where men hold most of the responsibility within the home's fiscal stability. They are pushed to earn higher educations, to make more money and care financially for their family's well-being. While that doesn't sound like a bad thing, it can be when the pressure to provide, serve and perform becomes too much, all while never being taught how to express yourself. When you've never been taught how to assert boundaries for your mental and emotional well-being. It's a culture that places high value in success—that the more successful you become it is because God is rewarding you for being a faithful servant and righteous steward.

Your purpose in life is to provide stability, leadership and exercise power over everyone and everything except your own mental and emotional health.

Now put a man in this position who has no desire to control other people. A man who is on the introverted side, who was never comfortable or even capable of emotional expression and vulnerability. A man who was given the responsibility to do everything for his wife and family, including earning an education and working to provide for them but was then criticized by his male peers and other high-ranking Mormon men for not fulfilling his priesthood duties. A man who converted to Mormonism in search of stability, not power. A man who bought into the expectation to provide but was drowning inside. It's like adding spoonfuls of baking soda to a glass beaker and after a few years you begin pouring in the vinegar by the gallons.

Suppress.

Suppress.

Suppress.

Then one day, *boom*!

This may not be the case for *all* LDS families, or *all* LDS men, but in my personal experience this was the narrative being enforced. So much so that our life was following that exact path the church had carved out for us when we found ourselves in that moment, on the bed, with Travis hitting rock bottom. Travis knew that while he was there with us, he wasn't really there at all. He realized that what we needed wasn't success, money or status— we just needed him. And while he was doing everything he could to provide for us with the weight of the world on his shoulders, all we wanted was access to his caring heart and loving soul.

Of course, I knew what it felt like to hit rock bottom. I'd been there not long before. And now, here we were together, united in the trenches of each other's souls—bound and determined to survive. We'd both hit our rock bottoms—in our marriage and as individuals.

For so long we had played by the rules—the church's rules. We had checked every box. We based all our decisions on the church's approval, the approval of our peers and we did everything we could to fit into the mold the church expected. We became toxic people pleasers, negligent of our own mental and emotional health, to be one with the hive—dedicating our lives to service, to the higher power.

Now, we were playing by *our* rules. We broke the mold. And we were left shattered, picking up the pieces together.

But this time, instead of becoming a shiny perfect example, we leaned into our brokenness and decided to live our life the best way we knew how—with honesty, integrity and a whole lot of love. Instead of putting the pieces back together, we picked them up, studied them closely and made conscious efforts to decide if these pieces belonged back in our lives, or if they were merely meant to belong to our past.

We began to live with intention. Our own intention. We allowed ourselves the space and freedom to explore who we really were as individuals and as a couple, with no restrictions. No churchy rules, no weaponized scripture, no living in fear of doing the wrong thing—just living, exploring, pondering and accepting or rejecting what felt true or false to us. Both of us were done conforming. Done. We were not going to continue to conform our lives around anyone or anything besides ourselves. This included conforming to each other. While I have always been supportive of being an individual within a marriage, this time, we were really going to explore what that meant. We were truly putting this concept to the test.

When you've been conditioned to think and act just like everyone else within your religious bubble for so long, individuality goes out the window. For us, not conforming to the other person meant having our own opinions on politics, religion, spirituality and dozens of smaller, everyday things. It meant giving the each other space *and* encouragement to explore things the other didn't understand. It meant that we didn't have to agree on everything all the time. And neither of us needed to ask permission to explore things that interested us. It meant not having to explain ourselves—ever again.

Once we started this journey to self-discovery, we realized that we never wanted to be forced into a situation where we were anyone but ourselves ever again. We wanted to live with authenticity and integrity and raise our son to do the same.

We also began to say "no" to toxicity. We set boundaries. We began to speak up and stand up for ourselves during times of mistreatment. We grew protective over each other and our little family. After all, we'd been through enough trauma. We'd been through religious abuse and years of manipulation. And after all that, we felt fiercely protective over the one thing we loved most—each other.

Through all of this, we began focusing on everyday joy, our emotional health, and what our next steps were as a family. We became uniquely and wonderfully ourselves. Like a fire-activated seed, covered in thick, impenetrable resin until it is burned away and forced to grow—we felt ourselves shifting, changing, sprouting. Although we were charred, the sticky beehive honey that had held us in the past had melted away, leaving us unbound and free. Free to fly.

And we were finally able to grow.

self-preservation

The teachings and culture of Mormonism
left me feeling more shame than
the love of Jesus.

"It's called 'self-preservation,'" she had said to me sympathetically. My first instinct was to deny this statement and correct her somehow, but I came up with nothing.

I adjusted my position on the lumpy couch where I sat, the cushions seemed to be swallowing me whole. She uncrossed her legs and leaned toward me in one effortless motion. I had only been seeing her for a few months but I loved her bluntness, her realness, and her presentness. Her energy had told me that she was genuine and kind, but I wanted her to be wrong about this. I was offended and in denial.

I had a good life. I had an amazing husband, a beautiful son, and more than most people could even hope for. She couldn't be right about this. She just couldn't be.

My mind searched—*reached* for a counter statement. Nothing. It was like my brain was in a dark, empty void with no words, thoughts or emotions. There was nothing for me to reach for, no excuse to come up with, no stupid joke to side-step, no reasoning beyond the truth. The truth that I was in fact in self-preservation mode and had been for years.

I smiled back at her... but it was the kind of smile that only pain knows. It was the quiet acceptance of sad truth. The submission to harsh reality.

155

Acknowledging this had felt like a stain on my illusion of perfection, or at least I perceived it that way. It had been five years since I had left the church and I still struggled with feelings of inadequacy, of failing and not being good enough.

During my years as a Mormon, I craved the approval of my church and the people in it—so much so, that I became a puppet, only moving when they pulled the right strings. I had felt mechanical, empty. My life was a series of checklists to prove my goodness. One wrong move and all eyes were on me… and not in the good way.

As Brené Brown said, *When perfection is in the driver's seat, shame is always riding shotgun.*

I explained to my therapist that was where I lived—in the shame. It didn't matter that I had left the church, my mind had been altered to expect perfection in the form of my ridiculous checklists and it was humanely impossible to check all the boxes. And this left me feeling like a constant failure, which led to overwhelming shame.

Even as I reflect on this experience all these years later, it brings me back to the constant stressors of everyday life as an active member. I remember speaking to other women my age and we'd agree how we felt inadequate in the church's eyes. How we weren't doing everything we should be doing. And how that made us feel. I realized through sharing my experiences that many people felt the same way as me, but the difference was that they'd never be caught dead speaking publicly about it. Those conversations were spoken in hushed voices behind closed doors.

Because there in the outspokenness lay a monster even bigger than shame. It is the shame of your peers, the shame of your family, and the ostracism of yourself from the only community you have.

In Mormon culture if your prayers aren't answered it's because *you* need more faith, or *you* haven't been good enough to deserve those blessings, or maybe *you* should go to the temple more to show God how devoted you are. Then He'll see that you deserve it. Or, what about that one time when you made out with your high school boyfriend and "went a little too far..." maybe that's why you aren't getting the blessings you're praying so hard for. You should probably go to your bishop to repent so God can forgive you. That's what it is.

Wait, one time you dropped a gallon of milk in the parking lot of an Albertsons and... I can't believe you said it, but you said, "fuck" out loud. You shouldn't have said that. You should ask God to forgive you for that. Shoot! Did you forget to read your scriptures yesterday? Yikes... better get home and do double the reading tonight to make up for it. Oh, and you totally forgot to do Family Home Evening on Monday, you're not being a very good example. Your family really needs that time to connect.

As juvenile as it sounds, all these micro "sins" leave you wondering if all of these little things over the course of your life will keep you out of heaven and away from your family forever. And it is really stressful because obviously you love your family. You need to be better so you can be with them for eternity.

And on it goes. It never stops. *Ever.*

Simply put, the teachings and culture of Mormonism left me feeling more shame than the love of Jesus. So much so that I found myself in yet another therapist's office to deal with the repercussions of over a decade of religious trauma and spiritual abuse.

And after I left my therapist's office that day, as she taught me about self-preservation and smashed every illusion of

157

perfection I had walked in there with, I had some serious unpacking to do. I'm talking mega-sized, over-filled, brought-too-many-souvenirs-home-from-vacay-and-had-to-buy-another-suitcase type of unpacking. The kind of unpacking you leave on your bedroom floor for weeks or months that gets shuffled around because you'd rather just move it out of the way rather than deal with the real problem.

Maybe you even stare at it from time to time and think, "Yeah, I should really unpack this. It's been five years." But then you make the choice to ignore it once again and go about your life—baggage unpacked, ready to be tripped over at a moment's notice.

Let me tell you something—when you finally trip over that unpacked baggage and fall flat on your face, you have no one else to blame but yourself. You can jump up and point your finger and yell at the baggage—hell, you can curse creatively in all your raging glory for all I care. But that's not going to change a damn thing. Baggage is the universal love language for a life lived.

Here's the thing, we've all got baggage. Especially the unpacked kind. And all of us have the choice to decide what we want to do with it. We can leave the baggage where it is. We can pile laundry on top of the baggage. We can shove the baggage under the bed—or we can unpack the baggage. Put it away. Sort it one delicate piece at a time.

What is in our baggage may not be in our control, but how we choose to deal with our baggage is completely in our control. Even when everything seems out of our control, it's not. Some of us, may need professional help unpacking it, others can do it independently—but all that matters is that we do it. We get to decide how to move forward. We get to decide who we are and how we show up. The baggage does not get to do that for us, unless we give it permission to trip us.

During this conversation with my therapist, I realized I was in complete denial—still living halfway in that truthful illusion we talked about earlier. After all, I'd left the church! I've moved on, healed, started my life over. How could I be in self-preservation mode years after I had left the toxic environment that caused me to feel so much shame?

The reality was that I had merely shoved that fully packed baggage full of all the shame and guilt and anger I'd ever felt in the darkest corner of my closet. Out of sight, out of mind. But like some demented jack-in-the-box, that puppy flung itself right open in the middle of my therapist's office. I couldn't run from it, hide it, or ignore it any longer. This baggage was mine and mine alone.

It had to be dealt with.

Once I came to the realization that I am the owner of my baggage and that it's my responsibility to unpack, there was a sense of power that took ahold of me. I could no longer run away from it, ignore it, or shove it into some dark corner somewhere. Maybe the contents of the baggage aren't entirely my doing but taking care of the baggage itself is mine and mine alone. What I choose to do with it is up to me. It's entirely in my control. No one else can snap their fingers and make it disappear—but I can be intentional about unpacking it one delicate piece at a time, handling it with care and attention. I can control how much time I want to take with each painful, traumatic piece of it. That alone was such a beautiful realization.

I think most of us ignore unpacking our proverbial baggage because we know that once we dive in, we may find some stuff that simply—sucks. We know that it's not going to be easy, that it's most likely not going to be quick, and it's definitely going to be painful and result in emotional exhaustion. Some pieces of your baggage will be intricately folded, placed right on top, easy to see, handle and put away. But others.... others will be caught in the zipper, so twisted and mangled beyond repair that you don't even remember what they looked like to begin with. These are the ones that matter the most.

My baggage was grief. I was grieving the community I'd left. I was grieving all the missed experiences of a free young woman who was not tamed by religion. I was grieving my illusion of perfection and the loss of Eunice's identity.

My baggage was also stress. The stress of becoming a Mormon woman and then trying to unbecome her. To erase her from every square inch of my life. The stress of becoming a mom so young and putting my whole self on the back burner for another. The terrifying realization that I made life altering decisions long before I had the maturity to deal with those consequences.

I came to realize I was caught in the zipper. I had so much baggage that I could not possibly begin to unpack, that I covered it up with work, ambition, goals, family, responsibility, and who knows what else. These things became my life raft. My safety net. Self-preservation at its finest. It became this throw your baggage in the creepy dark closet where Annabelle probably lives, ignore it, and give 1000 percent of yourself to everything else in your life so you simply don't have to deal with it. It's much easier to ignore your baggage when you stay busy. Because busy people don't have time to think. And thinking is scary and hard and sad. So, if you don't have time to think, you won't have time to feel. And on the cycle goes.

After a time, that so-called "life raft" sprung a leak and I was left floundering. As hard as I had tried to stay busy, my baggage eventually manifested itself into something much more complex—anxiety & depression.

The signs were there, but as I had gotten so accustomed to doing, I shoved it away and ignored it. Kept myself even more busy so I could forget. But the thing about mental illness is that you don't forget. It controls you. It sinks its claws into you like a barbed hook. I began to notice that I had no energy for things that used to bring me joy. My thoughts raced constantly. I stopped sleeping. I thought everyone hated me. I hated myself.

Per my therapist's suggestion, I made an appointment to see the doctor. The next thing I knew, I was sitting in a doctor's office filling out a survey.

In the last two weeks how often have you been bothered by the following problems: Little interest or pleasure in doing things? Check. *Feeling down, depressed or hopeless?* Check. *Feeling tired or having little energy?* Check. *Feeling bad about yourself or that you are a failure or have let yourself or your family down?*

Check.

Check.

Check.

Feeling afraid something awful might happen? Check. *Feeling nervous, anxious or on edge?* Check. *Not able to stop or control worrying?* Check.

Every day. All day. No matter what. Check.

That day I was diagnosed with clinical depression and general anxiety disorder. It's no surprise to me that I went from one checklist to another. One checklist was masked as the roadmap to eternal salvation, and the other... the other is scientifically proven to unveil a chemical imbalance that leads to mental illness.

One checklist was made by men claiming to be prophets, seers and revelators for all of mankind. This celestial checklist was the oppressor. The oppressor controls and manipulates and leaves the person empty as a shell. Because without the oppressor's checklist, there is nothing to be checked, nothing to keep track of your goodness and your worthiness. Nothing to tell you (or them) that you are good enough. The oppressor tells you that your worth is measured by the checklist. That your goodness is accounted for every time you complete a task masked in eternal salvation.

So, it should be no surprise that I found myself sitting in a doctor's office after leaving the oppressor with a new checklist. A checklist that told me right away that I was broken. That something was wrong with me. That somewhere along the way, when I was trying to prove my goodness and my enoughness, that it shattered me into a million pieces.

This checklist was based on science and made for people like me who were broken, tired and scared. It was made for a person like me who was manipulated and controlled for so long that I couldn't function without a checklist.

You see, eventually, the checklist of eternal salvation and toxic perfectionism changed my brain chemistry. It changed it so much that I convinced myself that everyone around me wanted me to fail. It changed so much that I started having heart palpitations and anxiety attacks. I stopped writing. I stopped enjoying my son's affection. I stopped longing for my husband's touch. I thought that maybe, just maybe, everyone I knew would be better off without me.

My constant up and downs were an inconvenience, I thought—they were a stressor to other people's lives. I was a stressor to everyone's life. And after I left the church, I felt free, but I also felt like I would never be enough. Ever. Like chewed gum on the sidewalk. Like once upon a time I had been great but over time I became unsavory, unwanted and spit out.

The worst part about it all is that I couldn't talk to any of my Mormon friends about the way I was feeling because I knew the answer they'd give me. I knew because I had thought the very same thing, once upon a time.

The answer was, "You can never know true joy without the church. You are feeling this way because you've been disobedient."

So, there I was. Stuck inside my own head. Between what I'd been conditioned to believe and what my soul told me was truth. I'd been conditioned to believe I was denying God's truth and could never feel true joy without the church, but my soul was telling me something different. My soul was telling me that I didn't believe God would punish me for leaving religion, because God was so much more than what religion made Him out to be.

God was within me.

I knew in the deepest parts of my soul that God, the universe, something bigger than me, knew me intimately. I knew that religion never defined my relationship with this omnipotent force. Yet, my brain—my orthodox conditioning—contradicted everything my soul, my intuition, the God within me, was telling me. But yet again, I chose to trust my own soul. I made a conscious choice to turn my back on the conditioning that had made me sick. I put my eternal salvation on the line to trust the God I felt inside of me. The God I knew was too big to fit into any man-made construct.

And this is how I began to unpack that baggage—by trusting myself. By getting professional help. And committing to moving forward—not just for myself, but for my son, for my husband, for us.

Not only did I deserve to live a life free from baggage, but they deserved to have a mom and a partner who valued herself enough to take care of it. They deserved a present, healthy person who adds dynamic value to the family unit.

The silver lining is that during this time I learned to lean into the relationships that made me feel safe. I leaned into my husband. I leaned into my mom. I leaned into my closest friends. Most importantly, I leaned into myself. I learned to trust myself, my intuition, and the divine presence within my own soul. I began to speak openly about my battles with depression and anxiety. I vocalized to those closest to me when I was having a "down" day and they graciously gave me space to deal with it however I needed to. There were, and still are, some days when I can barely get out of bed—though they are few and far between now that I've been proactive about my mental health. There are days when I ask my husband for tight hugs that make the anxiety feel bearable for a few moments. There are nights when I snuggle close to him and repeat, "I am safe and I am loved," until I can control my racing thoughts enough to fall back asleep.

Through this journey of healing, deconstructing and unpacking I began to wonder, if God is real wouldn't He want us to listen and trust ourselves? Like any loving parent, wouldn't God want us to feel safe in our divinity? Wouldn't God want to tear down the walls that make us small so we can be big and bold and limitless? Wouldn't God want us to actually live instead of just survive?

I began to believe that God would want what's best for me, even if that meant leaving "the one and only true church." I began to trust my own knowing that God would not want me to live by the checklists.

The checklists that led to my unraveling also led to my becoming. My unraveling had led me back to the desert where I played as a child. The desert where I was one with the jack rabbits. The desert that made me return home dirty, happy and reeking delightfully of Russian olive trees. The desert where Lindsay once thrived, and Eunice denied.

The desert where the wildness is dangerous but delicious to the taste.

free will

Free to fly, yet guided
by celestial force.

For my birthday, one year after I'd left the church, I got a tattoo—
a big one. This goes directly against the teachings I had been
taught my entire adolescence. The teaching that your body is a
temple and should be treated as such. Meaning, do not defile your
body with super cool artwork.

But it also goes beyond that. The teaching of "treat your
body as a temple" gave the church complete control over my body.
What I put in my body, on my body, used my body for—all of it
was decided by them, the 12 Mormon apostles and prophet of
God. The patriarchy. My body was merely a vessel of celestial
obedience. It became a symbol of how righteous I really was,
which is where the culture of the church gets really dark and ugly.

When I converted at 13-years-old, my body was my own.
I had complete ownership of it. My body exemplified no one but
me. Then suddenly, I was thrown into a world where my body
exemplified my willingness to comply to the strict teachings of a
religious organization and was told I was doing so in the name of
the Almighty. I was told that my body was given to me because I
was righteous in the pre-existence and that I needed to use my
body to do God's work here on earth. Any resistance to these
teachings was seen as defiance in the face of God.

Suddenly, my body became my enemy because of how
symbolic it was of my goodness.... of my "enoughness," of my
ability to be a righteous Mormon girl. Instead of waking up each
morning and simply existing comfortably as a young woman, I

was subjected to an inner checklist of determining my own worth. Was my skirt too short? Was my top too revealing? Was I going to get in trouble or judged if I drank that tea? Was I bad because I really wanted a second ear piercing or that I loved other people's tattoos? Would someone say something negative to me about wearing shorts and a tank top when I was exercising? What about that little peek-a-boo hole in my one-piece swimsuit—would I be asked to change?

To make it all worse, if I wore something deemed too revealing, the Mormon boys would shout, "modest is hottest!" as I walked by causing me intense shame and embarrassment. Everyone would laugh. These boys were celebrated for "Choosing the Right" and being "woke" to the ways of Satan and holding the girls around them accountable for keeping *them* righteous—for not tempting them with their bodies.

One of the first times I experienced this was after my high school homecoming dance. A few weeks prior, I found a gorgeous dress that my grandma agreed to buy for me. The only problem was that it was strapless. It came with a matching shawl, but I didn't want it to get in the way of dancing the night away. I just wanted to be carefree and have fun as any young woman would. My mom helped me find a seamstress who could make sleeves out of the fabric from the shawl and sew them onto the dress for me. During the appointment the seamstress took all my measurements with the dress on so she could create the perfect, custom cap sleeve.

On the day of Homecoming, I had my hair and makeup done professionally for the first time. I had never seen myself so done up with my hair in curls, and my almond eyes taking the stage as my most-loved part of myself. When I put on the dress, I felt like an actual princess. The dress was baby pink with a heavily beaded top and ruched bottom, with sparkling crystals in each fold. I found shoes that matched perfectly and bought extra crystals and fabric glue to add even more sparkle to my ensemble.

My Mormon date, one of my guy friends, was awestruck and fumbled over his words upon seeing me. We had the most magical night. I never wanted it to end. I felt like the most beautiful girl at the dance and my date confirmed that each time he looked at me.

On Monday, as I was leaving the seminary building, one of my girlfriends caught up to me and began walking to class alongside me.

"I didn't see you at the dance on Saturday," she said. "But I heard your dress was immodest." I stopped dead in my tracks. I furrowed my brow, confused.

"What are you talking about?" I said louder than I wanted.

"Yeah, I heard some of the girls talking and they said your dress didn't have big enough sleeves to cover your shoulders."

"Are you kidding me?" I shouted. "I had the dress altered to make sleeves! Why would they say that?"

I didn't give her time to answer. I stormed off to class and held back tears all day until I reached the comfort of my room at home. I sobbed and sobbed into my pillow. Then I grabbed the camera my mom had taken pictures of us with and looked at every single picture from that night to see where I had gone wrong. Then I determined that they were right. My sleeve was more of a wide tank top that still showed the upper crest of my shoulder. I was ashamed. I was embarrassed. I was wondering if everyone was talking about me and judging me and determining how good I actually was. If I really was a good Mormon girl.

Unfortunately, it didn't get better as I got older—It got worse as I grew into womanhood. After I was married and endowed in the temple, the church had ultimate authority over my body. After being endowed, I had to stay temple-worthy by participating in temple worthiness interviews with my bishop. He would then grant me an updated temple recommend, and then I could continue to go to the temple and buy underwear.

Yes, underwear.

After being endowed, members are required to wear temple garments which are symbolic of the fall of Adam, where he and Eve were suddenly aware of their nakedness and covered themselves. As an endowed woman, I was only allowed to take these garments off and be "naked" in the shower, during sex, and while wearing a modest bathing suit while swimming. Any other time, I was required to wear these sacred garments which covered the majority of my body underneath my clothing. They were never allowed to show. All clothing had to be modest enough to cover them, which meant high neck tops with the back, shoulders and belly covered, and long bottoms—nothing above the knee, and no holes showing the garments beneath.

The toxic culture within the church developed this saying called the "garment check." While garments needed to be covered at all times, there were opportunities for other members to see if endowed members were actually wearing their garments or not. All it takes is the right angle, or a young mom to bend down suddenly, awkwardly and inappropriately while wearing a skirt. All it takes is a shirt being just a bit too sheer or tight and the hem of the garment top can be seen.

By doing this "garment check" I could spot members of the church out in public, on vacation, and literally anywhere. It became a means to determine how good, how truly obedient a Mormon adult was. And I was just as critical as I was taught to be.

I became a product of my environment. I became the type of person that hurt my feelings after my first homecoming dance.

It wasn't until leaving the church that I became aware of my own learned toxicity. It wasn't until I left that I realized I had become the very person I despised. That was when I began my mission to find myself by practicing my own free will without guilt, without shame—just to be alive, wild and free.

Six months after I left, I came across a quote on Instagram by the poet Atticus. It read "Love her but leave her wild."

I adopted it immediately as my personal motto, as a quote that symbolized how I needed to be accepted by my loved ones. Then I decided I wanted my motto tattooed permanently on my body. The body that, for so long, had been controlled by men. The body that had not been mine for over a decade. The body that I was reclaiming as my own.

I was so excited.

When it was all said and done, I was in love with the piece and couldn't wait to share it. But I also felt like I couldn't, because my getting a tattoo meant I had defiled my body. And defiling my *own* body would cause negative emotions in *others*.

I was at a crossroads.

A few days later, I was talking to my therapist about it. I explained everything—all my emotions, my need to not upset anyone with my choices, how much anxiety I felt over making a decision that would cause others to be angry, how people might see me differently now that I was tainted. I felt fear and anxiety about losing love from others.

"What I am about to say might upset you, but I feel like you can handle it," my therapist said. "It's my job to be honest with you just as you've been honest with me. This behavior you are explaining tells me that you are a passively controlling person.

171

It isn't your fault, per say, it's just what you've been conditioned to become. You are so obsessed with making everyone else comfortable that you don't actually live for yourself."

My eyes went big. She was spot on. Then, I laughed a big boisterous laugh that made my therapist question if I was about to have a complete psychological breakdown. But she had just said the truest statement I had ever heard. And I knew that I had some serious work to do.

During my 10 years of Mormon conditioning, I learned that it is up to me to keep the waters silky smooth. Create no waves or disturbances. The love of my family and community is conditional on that fact alone. Only make choices that keep everyone but myself happy. Never question the church's authority or they will make sure to take that love away from me. I am not allowed to make life choices that will make them upset. Period. But keep smiling through it all because no one likes a frowner.

After a decade of quite literally living this way religiously, I found myself unpacking my passively controlling behaviors. My first step was to tell my mixed-faith grandparents about my new tattoo. Which meant telling my Mormon grandma.

Scary business.

They came to our house for a visit about a week after I'd gotten my tattoo. I was definitely going to tell them or maybe I'd just let them notice on their own? My tattoo is on my foot, it's large and hard to miss.

Five minutes prior to their arrival I panicked and ran up the stairs to our bedroom and put on the first pair of socks I found. I covered the potential disturbance. My need to passively control the situation was satiated. I sat on the bed and sighed in sweet relief. Like a hunger had just been met.

Knock, knock, knock.

Damnit to hell.

My fully covered feet sprinted down the stairs. I plastered a smile on my face and opened the door.

"Hello!" I shrieked through smiling teeth.

They stayed for an hour and never once did I take my socks off. I actually covered them further with a blanket from the couch. Hiding myself. Hiding my foot. Hiding something that made me happy all to appease the invisible force of passive control. And maybe out of fear that their love for me would change.

Ridiculous, I know.

After they left, I was disappointed in myself. I felt like I had done a lot of mental work, but when it came time to put it to the test I had failed. I had failed myself. And that hurt. So, a half hour after they left, I took my socks off, grabbed my phone and snapped a picture. Then I hit send, right to Grandma. Baby steps. I can't tell you with certainty whether they were upset, saddened, or angry, but I also didn't ask. I did not ask them to love it or even like it. I certainly did not ask for their opinion. To this day, I don't think they love it. But I know without a doubt that they love *me*. And that is what I needed. I needed to be allowed to make my own choices while still being loved without condition. I believe that is what *all* of us need.

But we also have to give up control in allowing others the free will to make choices that upset us. That we don't agree with. We are not always in the right. When the people we love make choices that evoke strong negative emotion, ask yourself, am I going to punish this person for exercising their right to free will *or* am I going to stay true to my emotion while still giving grace to this person I love dearly?

This is hard, I know it is. I have to practice this daily in my own relationships—most importantly with my husband and son. There is no perfect way to do this. But when you're struggling, tell the person you love that you need time to digest. Don't speak out of anger. Chew on the emotions. Chew on the facts. Dive into yourself to understand why their truth is causing that emotion. Create within yourself and your relationships a safe haven of love, exploration, forgiveness and understanding. Your free will permits you to do all of those things. It also permits you to do the exact opposite. But I promise that when you use your free will to heal yourself and love others, your life will be full of joy.

Through my faith deconstruction, I've used my own free will to explore. I've found truth, I've made mistakes, I've hurt people, and I've loved bigger than I've ever loved before. I've used my free will to discover who I truly am, and what I believe in without punishment or having the "fear of God" put into me. I've used my free will to allow myself to simply "be."

My awareness of practicing my own free will came to a head when I listened to spiritual author Ekhart Tolle speak for the first time. His words struck me so deeply and intimately I began to seek out his work. In an interview with *The Huffington Post*, Ekhart Tolle was asked, "Where do you think your spiritual journey is taking you next?"

"The mystic Hildegard of Bingen wrote that her path was to be 'a feather on the breath of God,'" he answered. "I aspire to that."

What a beautiful opportunity to free yourself of expectation and allow yourself to truly be a feather on the breath of God. Free to fly yet guided by celestial force.

Ever since I found these words, I have applied it to my own life. I have allowed myself to be a feather on the breath of God—fluid, free, yet guided and full of purpose. And I have allowed others the grace to do the same, because that is what I want for humanity—grace, love, freedom.

disappointment

If I spend my life chasing the validation I crave,
I am not truly living.
I'm simply running a marathon
that I will never win.

There's a familiarity about spending Christmas at my Mormon grandma's house that I cherish. I love watching my son roam the same rooms and hallways that I did growing up. I love watching him opening presents in front of the same windows, next to the same fireplace, surrounded by the same people that I was. In a small way it's like reliving my childhood. It's like living in a time before I became a "disappointment."

Often as children grow into adulthood we make choices that are different than the choices our loved ones would want for us. Sometimes, when we choose our own path it's not the path our family would've chosen for us. And most often the lens out of which we see the world is cut from a different source all together.

I truly don't believe anyone in my immediate family would think of me as a disappointment—however, it doesn't mean I've never felt like one.

One particular Christmas day, as we had finished cleaning up the Christmas wrapping wasteland my son tore through and left behind, my grandma sat next to me on her couch. I felt her weight through her eyes as she watched me intently. I could feel her words before she said them.

"So..." she started. "I wanted to tell you that I started listening to this minister on YouTube that is excellent. I really think you would like him... he doesn't shame anyone or make

177

anyone feel bad. He just quotes directly from the Bible. It's fantastic."

I felt a lump swell in my throat.

My Mormon grandma is someone I didn't want to disappoint but I knew my honest answer might do just that. Her influence has been heavy in my life, and I'd like to think my influence has played a heavy hand in hers as well. I am her only grandchild, after all. I lived with her my entire childhood and don't know what life is like without her. She is one of my biggest cheerleaders, and at times my most considerable critic. All of that sat heavy on my heart, knowing my honest response would feel like a gut punch to her.

I reached for my wine glass and took a nice, long sip. I swirled the dark cabernet around my tongue, taking in the notes of deep cherry, oak and spice. Her eyes were on me, awaiting my response. I could see the care and intentionality behind her blue-green eyes. I sensed the sensitivity in her voice. Finally, I swallowed the warmth that felt like the most glorious weighted blanket pushing the lump in my throat down ever so softly. My lips parted and I heard myself speak.

"That's so kind of you to think of me, Grandma," I said. "But to be honest, I don't find much comfort in the Bible anymore. It was used against me for so long. I would say I'm more spiritual than religious."

I heard the cliché of it the moment I had said it, but it was true. I am spiritual not religious. And to me, the Bible is not comforting. The thought of listening to a minister does not provide peace. At the same time, I feel so much joy that she finds strength and comfort in his words.

Perplexed, she shifted herself on the couch. She tilted her head with one eyebrow raised—thinking, confused, and turned to face me straight on.

"What does that mean? Spiritual?" she asked.

Across the room my mom was pretending not to listen, but I knew she is. She had that special ability all moms have where they pretend to be doing one thing but really their entire attention is focused elsewhere. Like having eyes in the back of her head.

I glanced at my uncle in the dining room adjacent to where we sit. He had absolutely zero clue what conversation was taking place and I wished that he would pass me the bottle of red sitting next to him. I sang silently to myself—take one down, pass it around, 99 feelings of dread in my heart! Then I looked into my grandma's eyes and explained my spirituality to her.

"I don't believe in putting God in a box. I don't believe the Bible accurately encompasses all that God is. I believe religion is a man-made concept created as a way to understand God, the universe, and all things unexplainable. I also believe religion and the Bible are man-made constructs that have been used to control populations of people for thousands of years. I believe in something bigger than myself and I guess I do refer to that as God, because I don't know what else to call it. But I don't believe God is a man or a woman or any one gender. I believe God is bigger than all that—which is why I also tend to refer to God as 'the universe.' I believe that whatever exists is for our good and *is* good. And with that, I give myself the freedom and permission to explore whatever magic exists in our universe for as long as I live."

There was a very long pause. A head tilt. A pair of wandering eyes that had told me her brain was trying to catch up to my words.

"Oh, okay," she finally said. Then her eyes light up as her brain translated all of this information to her. "Oh, I know what you are! You're a flower child! We had those in the sixties!"

I burst out laughing and brought my head down to my hands. I didn't object, but I didn't agree either. Honestly, I loved it. To her, I was speaking a foreign language and she was desperately making an attempt to understand. If I had to be defined as a flower child to make sense to her, I was fine with it.

"As long as you're not smoking pot I guess it's fine that you're a flower child," my grandma continued. My eyes widened, my eyebrows raised involuntarily, and I immediately reached toward my wine glass. I finished the remaining wine in one big gulp. In the same moment, my mom's head whipped around like in *The Exorcism of Emily Rose*, and she made eye contact with me as the wine burns down my throat.

I knew she was listening!

My mom then made a low throat clearing noise that sounded something like a dying goat. My grandma may be hard of hearing but she's not deaf. She heard the dying goat across the room and immediately turned to face my mom—her daughter. She saw the look on my mom's face, then whipped her head back around to face me.

"You're smoking pot!" she screamed.

The weight of my empty wine glass seemed unbearably heavy. Suddenly I wanted to drown myself in the sea of wrapping paper at my feet. I did nothing but stared at her blankly.

"What's that now?" I finally stammered.

"You're smoking pot?" she screamed again.

"Um... maybe a little. Sometimes. Occasionally. Not often. Barely."

My stepdad, who was two rooms away, somehow heard this entire interaction like some kind of bat with the echolocation skills of a sniper and decided now is a great time to contribute. He poked his head out of the kitchen with a cheeky look on his face.

"Just a *little*, huh?" he asked.

Fuck. Me.

I stared at my uncle across the room, who still had no idea what was going on and was within reach of the wine bottle. I shot lasers from my eyes into the back of his skull hoping to reach his soul for the sake of my own. If there was anyone to come to my rescue it would be him but he was as clueless as a fucking rock at this point. I rubbed my forehead, trying to think of some way out of this conversation. My husband's stifled laugh rang in my ears.

I immediately felt like a disappointment. Not only was I a post-Mormon, free-spirit flower child who referred to a genderless God as "the universe" and just denied all organized religion *and* the Bible, but now my Mormon grandma knew that I occasionally enjoyed an edible and smoked a little flower. I might as well have been a drug dealer.

Merry fucking Christmas, Grandma.

I felt both sad and proud that my illusion of perfection was suddenly gone. Like a weight had been lifted, but also that I may have just broken the heart of someone I love dearly. Someone who I brought back into the church 16 years ago. I had found the church on my own, and after I made the choice to be baptized my grandma fully embraced my new life path because it had been one she had been raised in. Something I never knew. And to my surprise, not only did she beam with joy at my baptism but she started attending church *with* me.

For years, every Sunday my grandma and I shared a hymn book, took the sacrament, and bonded over like-minded relationships in our ward. She soon held a calling as the ward librarian and I helped her before sacrament each week making copies, checking out materials, and organizing supplies. For the first time in my life, I felt a bond with someone close to me over spirituality—something I privately held close to my heart. It was a bond that I had never experienced in my life, until then.

Here's the thing that no one ever talks about—Mormon converts are completely alone and surrounded all at once. We are a singular force in our new religious community. We don't pile out of the minivan on Sunday morning with our baker's dozen to fill up a church pew. We don't go to adult Sunday school with our siblings or sing hymns as a family. We are one. And as well as the Mormon's embrace community, nothing can fill the emptiness of family. So, when my grandma rejoined the church, sat next to me every week and eventually went through the temple to receive her endowments, I got a slice of Mormon heaven right at my feet.

Then, there I was, sitting next to her on Christmas with my illusion of perfection being smashed to pieces. Part of me had felt liberated. The other part of me had felt ashamed. And of course, it all came back to control. I wanted to control my image around the ones I loved so I remain worthy of their love. And that day I felt I had lost all control. I was in my childhood home but I may as well have been under a microscope. Every orifice of my being was slowly but surely starting to show. I couldn't hide any longer. That meant showing the parts of myself that I didn't really want anyone to see. It meant being completely honest without holding back. What I wanted to say to her, my other family members, and friends of mine was that they might be disappointed. No, they *would* be disappointed.

As the peacemaker in my family my job has always been to lift others up, and sometimes that meant they didn't always get to see the terrible things I had to go through in my private life. Sometimes, I intentionally kept things from them because I knew that if I shared those things I would also share my pain. And being the empath that I am, the thought of that just about killed me. It also meant that I had a very hard time sharing every part of myself with them because, as the peacemaker, if I did something to upset them there was no peacemaker around to help *me* when I needed it. I have fought this "peacemaker mentality" for the last few years. It was not an expectation anyone else put on me. It was a learned behavior that turned into an expectation I put on *myself* as I grew into adolescence and then carried into adulthood.

But looking back to that Christmas, I am reminded that I am not in any way responsible for, or in control of, other people's emotions, thoughts or opinions. They own those. I do not. I also remind myself that other people do not own my right to have my own opinions, thoughts, feelings and versions of a story that may be different than theirs. I own those. They are mine. I give myself permission to have total ownership over myself—I own my heart, soul and every action and choice I choose to make.

In addition, I remind myself that I am not responsible for keeping other people, including my grandma or anyone in the outside world comfortable. If I make someone uncomfortable they are welcome to express their opinions, set boundaries, or choose not to include me in their lives altogether, because that is also a choice I have if need be. However, it is not my job to actively ensure everyone around me is good and comfortable and happy. As adults, they have ownership over those things—not me, not anyone else—except themselves.

So even though I admitted all of my questionable, closet post-Mormon behavior and beliefs to my grandma and felt like I was fucking everything up, I quickly remembered that as an adult she has the right and ability to make her own choices, have her own thoughts, establish her own beliefs and navigate her own feelings around everything I told her. She doesn't have to agree or give her stamp of approval. I relinquish the need for validation from her, and from everyone else in my life—because I would never truly live if all I did was chase after it. If I spend my life chasing the validation I crave, I am not truly living. I'm simply running a marathon that I will never win.

Just like my faith, my relationships are fluid. They are ever-changing, growing and morphing into something new. My need for control and stability doesn't always like this change, but eventually, I find the beauty in it.

Over the last few years especially, my relationships have changed vastly. My relationship with my grandma is different now than when I was an active LDS member. I've grown into a woman I am proud of and my grandma is proud of me too. It has been an experience of painful emotional evolution. Letting go of the religion that bonded us so tightly together during my formative years has been agonizing. Knowing that I was one of the only people that understood this part of her life is a welcome but excruciating experience. I love that she still shares her faith with me, but I hate that living my truth has caused an emptiness in her heart. One that she grieved for a long time. One that I grieved too.

Maybe feeling like a disappointment on that Christmas evening wasn't just that. Maybe it was me feeling disappointment because the era I cherished was truly coming to an end. No more smoke and mirrors. No more pretending and squishing into the boxes of perceived expectation. No more inauthentic ruses or hiding behind a kind smile. In that moment, I ended the era of being bonded by faith, and instead, stood on my own two feet,

independent, afraid and a little buzzed, bracing myself for a new
era to begin.

raising them

You don't know how to raise children
outside of religion because
no one taught you how.

Outside of overcoming RTS, healing from abuse, and recentering one's belief systems—raising children outside of religion is the number one question I see across the post-Mormon platforms. There seems to be a fear among parents that if they don't raise their children inside of religion, they are bound to fall into the wrong crowd or not have a strong sense of self without a Christian background.

To that I say, bullshit.

And also, give yourself some credit!

You are what your children need. You and all your uniqueness. You and all your flaws and mistakes and failures. You.

You may have been raised in a culture where the church "raised" the children, leaving the parents little to no choices in certain matters. Like deciding an age at which the child can date, go to school dances, what kind of movies they watch, music they listen to, etc. But that is *not* normal.

Let me repeat. *It is not normal.*

As parents our most difficult and debatably most rewarding job is having a hand in our children growing into good people, using the tools and values we worked hard to instill in them. Part of parenting is not having all the answers but following that intrinsic voice in your heart that directs your moral

187

compass—very well knowing you could screw them up at any minute but trying your best not to.

I will say, the nice part about parenting in the church is that there's a clear cut, well-worn path for most LDS children. You're born, you go to nursery, you become a Sunbeam, you get baptized, and then, when you enter Young Women or Young Men, you start your intensive "straight and narrow" training that leads to the temple, which leads to eternity.

Batta bing, batta boom. Takes a lot of the guesswork out of parenting, right?

Looking back on my teenage years, I realize that my mom lost up a lot of her control the minute I was baptized. She didn't know it of course, but the church was about to take total control of... everything. Suddenly they were the ones who decided what movies I could watch, the music I could listen to, the food I could eat, the liquids I drank, the clothes I could wear, my weekly schedule, my school schedule, the type of friends I could have, what core values I should have, my entire belief system. And so on and so forth.

In fact, I have a distinct memory of being in a Blockbuster on a Friday night with my mom when she picked up a new movie.

"Ohhh, I've really been wanting to see this one!" she said.

Feeling lucky they had one left to rent, we excitedly grabbed the DVD and hurried to the checkout counter. We paid and headed to the car. As I got my seatbelt on, my mom tossed the DVD into my lap like she'd done a thousand times. Except this time, the DVD landed upside down... you know the side with the rating on it. I glanced down and saw a big, bold "R" in the right-hand corner.

"Explicit content," it read. "Not suitable for children."

My heart sank. I was no longer allowed to watch R-rated movies. Even though my mom was okay with it, the church was not. I felt guilty. Guilty that I had just rented an R-rated movie and guilty that if I told my mom I couldn't watch it, she would be let down. I went completely silent during the car ride home as I felt my body become overwhelmed with anxiety. It was the first time I had been faced with the choice between my family, or them—the church.

For someone raised in the religion, it could be difficult to imagine living in a home where what you're taught goes directly against what you learn in church on Sunday. And most importantly, what you're raised within the church to believe you have to do in order to make it to heaven's pearly gates. But the thing is, for Mormon parents, the church has the final say in everything, leaving the parents to simply follow along. But this is not normal, and honestly, it's very intrusive.

The church likes control and it filters down into every detail of a person's life—including parenting. But the thing is, it starts slow and builds over time. Until before you know it, you've given them total control. Like a frog in boiling water—it doesn't know it's boiling to death if it dies nice and slow. Or, if it's all you know.

It pains me to see post-Mormon parents in such disarray over how to raise good children without religion having a say in any of it, because that tells me that they don't trust themselves to do the job. Like, without the herd and without the approval of the majority you're going to somehow mess them up. Or not do it the "right" way. Or somehow lead them into oncoming traffic and eternal hellfire.

Realistically though, the church is set up to operate as a "hive" mentality. The queen produces worker bees and the worker bees do nothing but serve the queen by supporting the rest of the hive. The queen continues to reproduce with the worker bees so she is always taken care of and the longevity of the hive is secured.

Sound familiar? Multiply and replenish the earth never sounded so sour.

When we allow another entity, another organization, to take over our parenting power completely we become nothing more than worker bees. We mindlessly work, day in and day out to secure the success of the hive. The system we are so dependent upon. The system that keeps us "safe." The system that has all the answers and tells us that we have a sacred duty to keep serving, keep doing, keep giving up our own power for the power of the hive.

Since leaving, I've had to take that power back. And I've had to learn what my parenting power is.

But here's the thing, we are all still children on the inside. We often replay our traumas, our successes, and our failures on our own children because we are just little 7-year-olds trying to make sense of all the fuckery happening around us. So, in that sense I understand how this could be very confusing—you've broken the cycle, you're ripping apart everything you've known to be true, and now you're left picking up the pieces. You don't know how to raise children outside of religion because no one taught you how. Because your mom and her mom before her— and on and on and on—all raised their children inside of religion and subsequently reenacted their childhood onto the next generation.

And now… now, there's you.

The different one. The one spreading her wings, leaving the hive and flying through uncharted territory where you get to make the rules. And it's terrifying.

So, how *do* we do it? How do we raise our children to be honest, kind, wholesome people outside of religion? How do we encourage independent thought while also instilling family expectations and standards of virtues we value? How do we teach our children about faith if we have none?

I don't know if I have answers to these questions, because, like you, I am still figuring it all out too. But what I do know is that people do it every day and have done it for thousands of years. Being good has *nothing* to do with religion. Living a wholesome, virtuous life has *nothing* to do with religion. Practicing honesty, integrity, and loving thy neighbor has *nothing* to do with religion.

But it does have *everything* to do with you.

At the end of the day, each of us makes choices. These choices either lead us toward the person we are proud to be, or not. Sometimes what we are meant to do with our life is outside the scope of what we are *taught* to be. And that's okay. We can blaze our own path for ourselves and for our children.

We should not be practicing high morals and virtues just because the church tells us to. We should be practicing them because that's what we want to contribute to our world, to our societies. For example, we should not be practicing integrity just because we are afraid of being caught if we are dishonest. We should be practicing integrity because that is who we are. Because being dishonest feels terrible on a soul-wrenching level. We should not be kind on the surface but cruel behind closed doors. We should not ask for forgiveness but refuse to forgive. We should not live a surface level life to sustain the good graces of our peers, instead we should be striving to live authentically with good intent, to make our world better.

It's okay to not have all the big picture answers as long as you're on a path that's teaching you. And if your children have that mentality, it will make their lives a whole lot easier. For one, they will learn to trust themselves—which is crucial. As we grow into adults, we become less and less teachable as we become set in our ways, but the key is to always remain open.

Open to possibility.

Open to new people, places and things.

Open to learning.

Open to a change of mind and heart.

Open to accepting and letting go.

Open to saying, "I'm sorry."

Open to listening.

Open to being wrong and changing our behavior.

I believe that everything we hope for our children begins and ends with us. We bring them into this world and have the insane opportunity to raise new life that can either make the world better or make it worse.

Here is what I feel is important to raising our children outside the parameters of religion:

Promote Independent Thought

Independent thought is not something that is endorsed within high control religions, so it is something many of us are lacking when we leave one. We are accustomed to the hive mentality. Follow the leader. Never ask questions and certainly never challenge anything. As adults this leaves us extremely malnourished in the self-trust department. We believe we simply cannot trust ourselves because we are "fallible humans," which we are but let's give ourselves some credit.

Our species has evolved and learned to survive throughout the eras and with thousands of belief systems in place.

When we lived as nomadic hunter-gatherers, we had to rely on our own instincts—not only for our own good, but for the survival of our kind. Every day we made crucial, possibly life-altering choices for the sake of survival. There weren't hundreds of thousands of us collectively deciding together what was right and what was wrong. We didn't have a queen bee prophet deciding what we should put into our bodies or how we spend our time. We had to experiment through trial and error.

We had to trust *ourselves* above all else.

And at the end of the day, it comes down to instinct, knowledge and self-reliance—all of which are normally not encouraged in high control religion. It's more about staying with the hive. The good of the group. The success of the organization. Being a faithful member who "doubts their doubts" before learning to trust themselves.

Remember the children's movie, *The Crood's*? The caveman family that does everything together? What does their daughter Eep want more than anything? She wants to be independent. To have her own opinions. To leave her pack and explore the terrifying, amazing world they live in—despite her father's wishes for her to stay put in their controlled environment. And what happens on the one night she decides to leave the pack? Well, a lot of scary stuff, but something else happens too.

Eep discovers fire.

For the first time in her existence, she feels the warmth, terror and beauty of a flame—something that will change the course of her and her family's life for the better. She doesn't know it yet, but things that were once considered toxic can now be edible, digestible and changed due to the heat of a simple flame. And even though her family is scared of it, tries to keep her away from it, and discourages it—Eep is drawn to it.

She is drawn to the light in the darkness, and her life is forever changed. Because of her persistence to remain true to herself, trust herself, and be brave—she changes the course of her life, and subsequently, her family's too.

Instead of trying to control our children's independence to fit our own narrative, we should be encouraging it. We should assist their independence by giving them mature direction and guidance as they navigate this beautiful and terrifying world.

It's important to remember that our children do not have the same world views as us. They do not wear the same historical lenses that we do. Therefore, they will not have the same opinions, values, expectations or beliefs as we do. By intentionally allowing our children to exercise their independence, make mistakes, and still be loved, we are teaching them a real-life lesson that maybe some of us missed out on growing up in the church.

The lesson that God loves us, but he is also just. The lesson that describes God as a loving father, and also someone to be feared in an eternal damnation kind of way. The hushed lessons we learned in the church hallways when we overheard who'd come home from their mission early or whose daughter wasn't getting married in the temple. The kind of lessons that teach us that there are conditions placed on the love we receive. And if you practice an ounce of independence that does not support the hive, then we will be thought of differently, rejected, unloved.

The thing is, respect and fear cannot exist in the same space. Allowing our children to practice critical thinking and independence, while being loved unconditionally is the most respectful thing we can do as parents. They will also learn to trust themselves and grow into adults who make decisions that are best for *them*.

It is no secret that our children teach us every day. And by granting them their independence they will have even more to show us, if we only let them.

Say I'm Sorry & Move On
My husband taught me this and I could not be more grateful. It is one of the most important lessons we've begun to teach our son.

I was raised in an environment where people were angry and stayed angry for days. Slamming doors and screaming matches followed by the silent treatment were a very regular occurrence. And when we first got married, that's the only way I knew how to argue.

Travis came from a home where he didn't see much arguing but one day his parent's marriage was just… over. Which left him feeling really confused.

After Travis and I had been married for a year or two, I realized I had complete control over how I wanted to disagree—and I decided I didn't want to disagree like I had been taught. I didn't want to continue the cycle of fighting without truly speaking. Arguing without reaching a conclusion. It was like playing a game of my dick is bigger than your dick—it was pointless and fueled by ego.

I wanted to fight better. I wanted to fight without feeling like my marriage was going to end or being left feeling like I had a hole in my stomach from all the blows I'd dealt. I wanted to fight without really fighting at all. I wanted to be able to express myself without fighting words. I wanted to feel respected while also respecting the person at hand. I wanted to get to forgiveness and move on.

As Beckham grew, I realized I never wanted him to feel like he was unlovable or unforgivable. I wanted to be able to express myself but also allow space for him to do the same in return. I wanted to be able to express my frustration with love and even a conversation where we both share our feelings. I wanted to be that example to him so that as he grows into a man he can communicate and express himself in a healthy, beneficial way that will hopefully lead to lasting relationships in his life.

Forgiveness goes hand in hand with love. And that is what I want for Beckham. That's what I want for us. If we are unable to forgive, how are we able to love? There is no way. Not fully. Because our love is being clouded by anger, defensiveness and ego. Being able to communicate our anger and frustration and apologize has been huge for my own personal growth and for the cohesiveness of our family unit.

Something that Travis and I do with Beckham is we talk about everything. We are honest in our communication with him. We try really hard to talk things out, give each other space and allow each other the freedom to express themselves. Then we move on. We work hard at not holding onto our anger—and we shouldn't have to if we are navigating it in a way where everyone feels heard, respected and loved.

I believe forgiveness to be a deeply profound and personal concept for each relationship—whether it is friendship, familial or romantic. I also think it is something hard to teach, unless it is taught by example.

Growing up in the church we are taught to look to Jesus as the shining example of forgiveness, yet it is not practiced in our congregations, in our homes, or within our own hearts. The church didn't just punish us for making "bad" choices, they shamed us. They shamed us by holding our worth over our heads in a very public way. And the only way we can break free of this cycle is to practice forgiveness earnestly with intent to make our homes and our world a more loving place.

Create a Safe Landing Space

I picked my son up from soccer camp one day and as soon as he saw me his shoulders slumped, he dragged his feet and started to whimper.

"What's wrong?" I asked.

"I'm so tired, Mommy. My feet hurt and I'm so hot," he said solemnly. Moments before, I had watched him cheerfully run into a circle with other children and do their end of day cheer. But once he laid eyes on me he became an ocean of emotion.

To be honest, sometimes this kind of thing frustrates me. I want to reap the benefits of doing what good parents do by putting their kid in fun summer camps. The benefit of seeing him happy and thriving. The benefit of watching him learn new skills and make new friends. The benefit of knowing that he's not on the iPad or watching television while I am working from home. But then I remind myself that I am his safe space. Once he lays eyes on me, he knows he can tell me what he's really feeling.

After we had made it to the car that day, he climbed into his car seat and I unlaced his cleats. Moments later, he was asleep. Later that day I was finally able to ask him how soccer camp was going and he told me all about it. The good, the challenging, and the not so good.

There are moments in parenthood when I get disappointed because I put my expectations of what certain things should be like before the feelings and needs of my child.

My expectation is that soccer camp would be *fun*.

Exercise.

Friends.

Soccer.

Socialization.

Screen-free.

Three blissful hours to myself!

And when I was met with slumped shoulders, whining and an overall "done with the day" attitude, my expectations were not validated and I was disappointed. But when I let him decompress, take a little nap and rest, I found out he *did* have fun. And I also learned that he was challenged in new ways and was met with some social situations he needed help navigating.

Creating a safe space sometimes means throwing your expectations out the window. Our children are experiencing everything for the first time, and that is often overwhelming. Even if it is fun, it is new and different and they need a safe space to decompress. This example is such a small one, but I know big important moments are coming where I will have to put this to the test. Because at some point our children fly the coop and only come home to eat and sleep. And while they're out living their lives, a lot of things can and will happen. It's important they feel their home is their safe landing space. Like when they come home they can feel the love, security and trust that we *all* need no matter what happens out "there."

If there is anyone or anything (including toxic traits and learned behavior that hurts others) in your home or in your life that makes your children feel unsafe—get rid of it. Take out the trash. Kick it to the curb. Your children's health and safety are the number one priority. Breaking unhealthy and unsafe cycles begins with you. You have the control to make this happen, so ensure it does.

Showcase Intrinsic Confidence & Self Love

This one is a tough one. I can tell you right now that I don't always feel like sunshine and rainbows on the inside. I don't always love myself. I don't always feel confident. But our children watch our habits.

Do we eat healthy? Exercise? Take care of our hygiene, mental health and our spirits? How we show up and take care of ourselves gives our children a sense of self love. After all, we must love the things we care for, right? And if we are mindful to take care of ourselves, that is showing our children what it looks like to practice self-love.

Intrinsic confidence means confidence that comes from within you—not from an external source. As far as intrinsic confidence goes, everyone is different. I have certain stages of my life that I've really struggled—like when I was training for my black belt in Tae Kwon Do and my body looked a lot different than the other girls my age. My thighs were thick and muscular, and my shoulders were defined. I was also a late bloomer of sorts and didn't develop at the same rate as my female peers. I felt very insecure about my body, as most teenagers do. I felt ashamed to take up too much space or be too muscular or just be too much in general. I wanted to simultaneously be seen and loved while being as unnoticeable and distanced as possible.

It's all part of growing up. Feeling insecure, scared and unsure is totally normal. But eventually, you grow out of it and discover who you are. Some of us get there quicker than others, but all that matters is that we are moving forward.

When I became a mom, it was like a snake shedding her skin. I grew, uncomfortably so, but I completely transformed. I struggled with self-love, much like I did when I was a young athlete navigating puberty. This time I was an adult woman with a child, learning how to love her new body, her new role and her new life. And I was bound and determined to be an example of self-love and intrinsic confidence to my baby boy. I wanted him to not just see me as his mom but as a person with goals, talents, shortcomings and failures. And I wanted him to see me rise and fall and love myself through it all.

Although Beckham doesn't remember it, he was there through my faith transition and during my becoming. He was an integral part of all of it! He watched his mom go to therapy. He saw the woman that gave him life break down and rise up again. He sees her make mistakes every day and apologize and attempt to do better. He watches his parents communicate and love deeply. His life is not perfect. Our life is not perfect. But we love ourselves and we love each other.

When I have love for myself and a sense of inner confidence, I can love others on a deeper level. I no longer need external validation, acceptance or attention to feel love for myself. While those things still feel good, they are not the foundation in which my identity is built upon.

While I was still an active member in the LDS church, my identity solely relied on all of those things because the culture of the church supported it. The culture of the church supports the idea that without them, you're nothing. That without the church, you're lost.

Would you ever want your child to feel that way? Or would you rather they have a deep self-love that no one could ever take away?

I had a huge shift in my mindset post Mormonism. I started practicing certain things that made me feel love for myself, that also made me feel powerful and happy. I practice my own self-love and develop my intrinsic confidence by making independent decisions and setting boundaries without approval from the majority. By not actively or routinely seeking out validation from external sources. By finding happiness in the little things. By learning a new skill, hobby or sport, just because I want to—that does not involve the family or church. By expressing to Beckham that I don't have all of life's answers and that I'm still learning, too.

I allow myself the freedom to explore my own soul in the pages of my journal or in my own private thoughts. I think deeply about many things and take time to ponder them. I take care of my physical health by staying active, eating a healthy-ish diet, and taking anxiety and depression medication daily.

We can't expect our children to learn intrinsic confidence and self-love if we ourselves are not showcasing those attributes. Sometimes it is incredibly difficult. After all, we are our own worst critic. Add some religious trauma and you've got yourself a self-loathing sundae with a cherry on top.

I encourage you to journal, reflect, create, read, listen or do whatever feels good in your soul. That is where you will find yourself. Just like your child will not truly find himself swimming in a sea of sameness with his peers, neither will you.

Sometimes, being true to yourself means being brave enough to love yourself as you blaze your *own* path.

independent decisions and setting boundaries without approval from the majority. By not actively or remotely seeking our validation from external sources. By finding happiness in the little things. By learning a new skill, hobby or sport, just because I want to—that does not involve the family or church. By expressing to Beckham that I don't have all of life's answers and that I'm still learning, too.

I allow myself the freedom to explore my own soul in the pages of my journal or in my own private thoughts. I think deeply about many things and take time to ponder them. I take care of my physical health by staying active, eating a healthy-ish diet, and taking anxiety and depression medication daily.

We can't expect our children to learn intrinsic confidence and self-love if we ourselves are not showcasing those attributes. Sometimes it is incredibly difficult. After all, we are our own worst critic. Add some religious trauma and you've put yourself a self-loathing sundae with a cherry on top.

I encourage you to journal, reflect, create, read, listen or do whatever feels good in your soul. That is where you will find yourself. Just like your child will not only find himself swimming in a sea of sameness with his peers, neither will you.

Sometimes, being true to yourself means being brave enough to love yourself as you blaze your own path.

ABOUT THE AUTHOR

Lindsay is an ex-convert of the Church of Jesus Christ of Latter-Day Saints (LDS), also known as the Mormon Church. She obtained her bachelor's degree at Brigham Young University-Idaho, where she met her husband. They were later married in the Columbia River Washington LDS Temple in Richland, Washington. Together they started their family and left the LDS church, starting life anew. Lindsay now lives with her husband and son under the shadow of Mt. Rainier in western Washington state.

AuthorLindsayHelm.com.
Instagram: @linds.helm
Facebook: @lindsayhelmwriter

Elisely Publishing is a woman-owned boutique publishing company on a mission to create global impact through building community. Our authors share their life experiences and professional knowledge to ignite transformation that creates community where it's needed most, offers hope by casting light into the darkest corners of the globe, gives a voice to those who are momentarily left voiceless, and builds a foundation of bravery for future generations.

Elisely.com
Instagram: @elisely.publishing
Facebook: @EliselyPublishing